THE THREE BATTLEGROUNDS

FRANCIS FRANGIPANE

The Three Battlegrounds

Copyright © Francis Frangipane
First Edition 1989
Revised Edition 2006

41st printing, July 2011

ISBN-13: 978-1-886296-38-1
ISBN-10: 1-886296-38-3
Printed in the United States of America
All rights reserved

Arrow Publications, Inc.
P.O. Box 10102
Cedar Rapids, IA 52410
Phone: (319) 395-7833
Toll Free: (877) 363-6889 (U.S. only)
Fax: (319) 395-7353
Web: www.arrowbookstore.com

CONTENTS

PREFACE

We would encourage our readers to become familiar with the glossary in the back of this book. Also, from time to time we update our text. If you see some things differently than we do, please let us know. As the Lord leads, we will make necessary revisions in a subsequent printing.

No one is more mindful of the fact that we are exploring uncharted regions of a subject that is ever unfolding. There is yet much wisdom and knowledge to discover in these dimensions. Therefore, let us approach these studies being mindful of our present inadequacies.

At the same time, this volume will serve as a companion for those serious leaders and prayer warriors who earnestly desire to become conformed to Jesus Christ. As we pass to you our information, our confidence is that the Lord Himself has set His heart to guide us. In Him, all things are complete, and by relying upon Him all things become adequate.

INTRODUCTION

This is a book about spiritual warfare. Before we proceed, however, I have two concerns. The first is our need for wisdom. There is an old European proverb worth heeding. It reads: *"Age and treachery will always defeat youth and zeal."* Before we engage in spiritual warfare, we should know this about Satan: he is an ancient and extremely treacherous foe. On the other hand, the strength of most Christians lies primarily in idealism and untested fervor. It is not long, usually five to ten years in the ministry, and most zeal has waned. Without warning, the minister's call has deteriorated from a walk of vision to a mere job.

What occurred was that zeal, by itself, challenged the treachery of hell and lost. The brightness of youthful dreams dimmed under the dark cloud of relentless satanic assault. Under the weight of growing frustrations and discouragement, compromise increased, and with it came iniquity and spiritual bondage.

Yet, the real villain was not sin but ignorance. We put the devil in a doctrinal box and expected him to stay there. He did not. He undermined relationships, and our love grew cautious. He resisted us in prayer, and our faith turned weak. Disillusion-ment set in. After spending much time with struggling pastors, I have seen a common trend in most: *They failed to discern the assault of the devil.* They stood unprotected against an ancient, treacherous foe.

Jesus prepared His disciples for everything, including spiritual warfare. They watched Him cast out demons; they clearly knew the devil was real. In fact, He sent them forth to also deliver people from demons. But before He sent them out, He charged them to become wise "as serpents" yet innocent and harmless "as doves" (Matthew 10:16). This fusion of divine *wisdom* and Christlike *innocence* is the taproot of all spiritual victory. Indeed, we can defeat the enemy, but wisdom must precede warfare and virtue must come before victory.

Consequently, the goal of this book is to train the church in wisdom and call the church to innocence. We will not disregard what we have previously learned; we will still live by faith. But we must learn the ways of God, which means we must think with wisdom. And we must be pure of heart, that we may see God and gain discernment. Indeed, it is the lack of discernment that has left us vulnerable to satanic attack.

Of my second concern, let me say that there are no shortcuts to successful warfare, only ways to make it longer and more perilous. One way of peril is to enter battle blinded by presumption. When it comes to waging war effectively, consider carefulness to be the essence of victory.

Whatever lofty spiritual plane you imagine that you are on, remember: Adam was in *Paradise* when he fell. Before your increased knowledge and religious experiences make you overly self-confident, recall that Solomon wrote three books of Scripture; *he actually gazed upon the glory of God,* yet he fell. Yes, even in your deepest worship of the Almighty, do not forget in long ages past *Lucifer himself was once in heaven* pouring out praise to God.

We each know of many who have fallen. Jesus warned that the love of many would grow cold. Do not presume it cannot happen to you. Our enemy has been deceiving mankind for thousands of years. Our experience, on the other hand, spans but a brief moment. It is wisdom to recognize that we do not know all there is to know concerning warfare.

Therefore, be bold but never brash or arrogant in your prayer life. Use your spiritual authority administratively, compassionately, but never presumptuously. Multitudes of well-meaning but ignorant Christians have approached the field of spiritual battle with flippant attitudes and have suffered greatly for it. Study several books and seek confirmation from the Lord for your strategies. As it is written, "Prepare plans by consultation, and make war by wise guidance" (Proverbs 20:18).

Thus, our purpose here is to help equip you for battle in three primary areas of battlegrounds: the mind, the church and the heavenly places. There are other fields or subcategories of spiritual warfare; however, these are where most of us will face conflict.

One last note. A few of you will be instrumental in actually saving your cities. Our prayer is that these chapters will help guide and equip you for that goal. The promise of the Spirit speaks thus: "There was a small city with few men in it and a great king came to it, surrounded it, and constructed large siegeworks against it. But there was found in it a poor wise man and he delivered the city by his wisdom" (Ecclesiastes 9:14–15).

While many are predicting the destruction of our nation and the collapse of our cities, they have not considered the power of *Christ in you.* But remember, "Wisdom is better than strength . . . wisdom is better than weapons of war" (Ecclesiastes 9:16, 18).

—Francis Frangipane, July 1989

PART ONE

THE

BATTLEGROUND

OF THE MIND

You will remember that the location where Jesus was crucified was called "Golgotha," which meant "place of the skull." If we will be effective in spiritual warfare, the first field of conflict where we must learn warfare is the battleground of the mind; i.e., the "place of the skull." Indeed, the territory of the uncrucified thought-life is the beachhead of satanic assault in our lives. To defeat the devil, we must be renewed in the spirit of our minds!

CHAPTER 1

SATAN'S DOMAIN: THE REALM OF DARKNESS

Many Christians debate whether the devil is on the earth or in hell; can he dwell in Christians or only in the world? The fact is, the devil is in darkness. Wherever there is spiritual darkness, there the devil will be.

PREPARING FOR SPIRITUAL WARFARE

For most, the term *spiritual warfare* introduces a new but not necessarily welcomed dimension in their Christian experience. The thought of facing evil spirits in battle is an unsettling concept, especially since we came to Jesus as lost sheep, not warriors. Ultimately, some of us may never actually initiate spiritual warfare, but all of us must face the fact that the devil has initiated warfare against us. Therefore, it is essential to our basic well-being that we discern the areas of our nature which are unguarded and open to satanic assault.

Jude tells us, "And angels who did not keep their own domain, but abandoned their proper abode, He has kept in eternal bonds under darkness for the judgment of the great day" (Jude 1:6).

When Satan rebelled against God, he was placed under eternal judgment in what the Bible calls "pits" (2 Peter 2:4) or "bonds" of darkness. The devil and the fallen angels with him have been relegated to live in darkness. This darkness does not simply refer to areas void of visible light. The eternal darkness to which this Scripture refers is essentially a *moral* darkness, which ultimately degrades into literal darkness. However, its cause is not simply the absence of light; it is the absence of God, who is light.

It is vital to recognize that this darkness to which Satan has been banished is not limited to areas outside of humanity. Unlike those who do not know Jesus, however, we have been delivered out of the domain or "authority" of darkness (see Colossians 1:13). We are not trapped in darkness if we have been born of light. But if we *tolerate* darkness through tolerance of sin, we leave ourselves vulnerable to satanic assault. For wherever there is willful disobedience to the Word of God, there is spiritual darkness and the potential for demonic activity.

Thus Jesus warned, "Take heed therefore that the light which is in thee be not darkness" (Luke 11:35 KJV). There is a light in you. "The spirit of man is the lamp of the Lord" (Proverbs 20:27). Your spirit, illuminated by the Spirit of Christ, becomes the "lamp of the Lord" through which He searches your heart. There is indeed a holy radiance surrounding a true Spirit-filled Christian. But when you harbor sin, the "light which is in thee" is "darkness." Satan has a legal access, given to him by God, to dwell in the domain of darkness. Thus, we must grasp this point: *The devil can traffic in any area of darkness, even the darkness that still exists in a Christian's heart.*

GOD'S THRESHER

An example of Satan having access to the carnal side of human nature is seen in Peter's denial of Jesus. It is obvious that Peter failed. What we do not readily see, however, is what was occurring in the invisible world of the spirit.

Jesus predicted accurately that Peter would deny Him three times. Anyone looking at Peter's actions that night might have simply concluded his denial was a manifestation of fear. Yet, Peter was not fearful by nature. This was the disciple who, a few hours earlier, drew a sword against the multitudes who had come to arrest Jesus. No, human fear did not cause Peter to deny the Lord. Peter's denial was satanically induced.

Jesus had warned the apostle, "Simon, Simon, behold, Satan has demanded permission to sift you like wheat; but I have prayed for you, that your faith may not fail; and you, when once you have turned again, strengthen your brothers" (Luke 22:31–32). Behind the scenes, Satan had demanded and received permission to sift Peter like wheat. Satan had access to an area of darkness in Peter's heart.

How did Satan cause Peter's fall? After eating the Passover, Jesus told His disciples that one of them was going to betray Him. Scripture continues, "They began to discuss among themselves which one of them . . . was going to do this thing" (Luke 22:23).

This was a very somber time. Yet, during this terrible moment, "there arose also a dispute among them as to which one of them was ... greatest" (Luke 22:24). They went from an attitude of shock and dismay to an argument concerning who among them was the greatest! Evidently Peter, the water-walker, who was also the boldest and most outspoken of the apostles, prevailed. We can imagine that Peter's high visibility among the disciples left him with an air of superiority, which was fanned by Satan into an attitude of presumption and boasting. Peter, being lifted up by pride, was being set up for a fall.

Pride caused Satan's fall, and pride was the very same darkness manipulated by Satan to cause Peter's fall. Lucifer, from experience, knew well the judgment of God against religious pride and envy. He knew personally that pride goes "before a fall" (Proverbs 16:18 KJV). Satan did not have a right to indiscriminately assault and destroy Peter. He had to secure permission from Peter's Lord before he could come against the young apostle. But the fact is, the devil demanded permission to sift Peter, and he received it.

SUBMIT TO GOD

The trip wire that Satan used to cause Peter's fall was the disciple's own sin of pride. *Let us recognize before we do warfare that the areas we hide in darkness are the very areas of our future defeat.* Often the battles we face will not cease until we discover and repent for the darkness that is within us. If we will be effective in spiritual warfare, we must be discerning of our own hearts; we must walk humbly with our God. Our first course of action must be, "Submit ... to God." Then, as we "resist the devil ... he will flee" (James 4:7).

Satan will never be given permission to destroy the saints. Rather, he is limited to sifting us "like wheat." The good news is that God knows there is wheat inside each of us. The outcome of this type of satanic assault, which is allowed through the permissive will of God, is to cleanse the soul of pride and produce greater meekness and transparency in our lives. It may feel terrible, but God causes it to work for good. Our husk-like outer nature must die to facilitate the breaking forth of the wheat-like nature of the new creation man. Both the chaff and the husk were necessary; they provided protection for us from the harsh elements of this life. But before God can truly use us, in one way or another we will pass through a time of threshing.

Peter's husk nature was presumptuous and proud. His initial successes had made him ambitious and self-oriented. God can never entrust His kingdom to anyone who has not been broken of pride, for pride is the armor of darkness itself. So, when Satan demanded permission to assault Peter, Jesus said in effect, *You can sift him, but you cannot destroy him.* The warfare against Peter was devastating but measured. It served the purpose of God.

Peter was ignorant of the areas of darkness within him, and his ignorance left him open to attack. But the Lord would ask each of us, "Do *you* know the areas where you are vulnerable to satanic assault?" Jesus would have us not be ignorant of our need. In fact, when He reveals the sin in our hearts, it is so He might destroy the works of the devil. Thus, we should realize that *the greatest defense we can have against the devil is to maintain an honest heart before God.*

When the Holy Spirit shows us an area that needs repentance, we must overcome the instinct to defend ourselves. We must silence the little lawyer who steps out from a dark closet in our minds, pleading, "My client is not so bad." Your "defense attorney" will defend you until the day you die—and if you listen to him you will never see what is wrong in you nor face what needs to change. For you to succeed in warfare, your self-preservation instincts must be submitted to the Lord Jesus, for Christ alone is your true advocate.

We cannot engage in spiritual battle without embracing this knowledge. Indeed, James 4:6 says, "God is opposed to the proud, but gives grace to the humble." God is opposed to the proud. That is a very important verse. If God is opposed to the proud, and we are too proud to humble ourselves and admit when we are wrong, then God is opposed to us.

James continues in verse 7, "Submit therefore to God. Resist the devil and he will flee from you." When we see this verse, it is usually all by itself as a monument to spiritual warfare. However, it is in the context of repentance, humility, and possessing a clean heart that we find Satan fleeing from us.

We must go beyond a vague submission to God; we must submit the exact area of our personal battle to Him. When we come against the power of the devil, it must be from a heart in submission to Jesus.

There is a recurring precept throughout this book. It is vital that you know, understand, and apply this principle for your future success in spiritual warfare. That principle is this: *Victory begins with the name of Jesus on your lips, but it will not be consummated until the nature of Jesus is in your heart.* This rule applies to every facet of spiritual warfare. Indeed, Satan will be allowed to come against the area of your weakness until you realize God's only answer is to become Christlike. As you begin to appropriate not just the name of Jesus but His nature as well, the adversary will withdraw. Satan will not continue to assault you if the circumstances he designed to destroy you are now working to perfect you.

The outcome of Peter's experience was that, after Pentecost, when God used him to heal a lame man, a new, humble Peter spoke to the gathering crowd. He asked, "Why do you gaze at us, as if by our own power or piety we had made him walk?" (Acts 3:12) Peter's victory over pride and the devil began with the name of Jesus on his lips, and it was consummated by the nature of Jesus in his heart. The darkness in Peter was displaced with light; the pride in Peter was replaced with Christ.

CHAPTER 2

THE STRONGHOLD OF THE GODLY: HUMILITY

Satan fears virtue. He is terrified of humility; he hates it. He sees a humble person and it sends chills down his back. His hair stands up when Christians kneel down, for humility is the surrender of the soul to God. The devil trembles before the meek because, in the very areas where he once had access, there stands the Lord, and Satan is terrified of Jesus Christ.

WHO TRULY ARE YOU FIGHTING?

You will remember that, at the fall of man in the Garden of Eden, the judgment of God against the devil was that he should eat dust (see Genesis 3:14). Remember also that God said of man, "you are dust" (Genesis 3:19). The essence of our carnal nature—of all that is carnal in nature—is dust. We need to see the connection here: Satan feeds upon our earthly, carnal nature of "dust." Satan dines on what we withhold from God.

Therefore, we need to recognize that the immediate source of many of our problems and oppressions is not demonic but fleshly in nature. We must contend with the fact that one aspect of our lives, our flesh nature, will always be targeted by the devil. These fleshly areas supply Satan with a ready avenue of access to undermine our prayers and neutralize our walk with God.

It is only our exaggerated sense of self-righteousness that prevents us from looking honestly at ourselves. As Christians, we know the Holy Spirit dwells within us, but we must also become aware of where we are tolerating sin if we will be successful in our war against the devil. Therefore, be specific when you submit yourself to God. Do not rationalize your sins and failures. *The sacrifice of Jesus Christ is a perfect shelter of grace enabling all men to look honestly at their needs.* Accordingly, be honest with God. He will not be horrified or shocked by your sins. God loved you without restraint even when sin was rampant within you; how much more will He continue to love you as you seek His grace to be free from iniquity?

Before we launch out in aggressive warfare, we must realize that many of our battles are merely the consequences of our own actions. To war effectively, we must separate what is of the flesh from what is of the devil.

Allow me to give you an example. My wife and I once lived in an area where a beautiful red cardinal kept its nest. Cardinals are very territorial and will fight off intruding cardinals zealously. At that time, we owned a van which had large side mirrors and chrome bumpers. Occasionally, the cardinal would attack the bumpers or mirrors, thinking his reflection was another bird. One day, as I watched the cardinal assail the mirror, I thought, "What a foolish creature; his enemy is merely the reflection of himself." Immediately the Lord spoke to my heart, "And so also are many of your enemies the reflection of yourself."

Before we have any strategy for attacking Satan, we must make sure that the real enemy is not our own carnal nature. We must ask ourselves, *Are the things oppressing us today the harvest of what we planted yesterday?*

AGREE WITH THINE ADVERSARY

You will remember that Jesus taught:

Agree with thine adversary quickly, whiles thou art in the way with him; lest at any time the adversary deliver thee to the judge, and the judge deliver thee to the officer, and thou be cast into prison. Verily I say unto thee, Thou shalt by no means come out thence, till thou hast paid the uttermost farthing.   —Matthew 5:25–26 KJV

Jesus is speaking here of more than avoiding lawsuits. In fact, He speaks in such a way as to indicate that, in regard to this particular adversary and this particular judge, we will always lose our case and end up in prison.

This parable explains God's view of human righteousness. In the narrative, the adversary is the devil and the Judge is God. Satan, as our adversary, stands as the accuser of the brethren before God, the Judge of all. The truth Christ wants us to see is that when we approach God on the basis of our own righteousness, the adversary will always have legal grounds to "cast [us] into prison," for our righteousness *is* "as filthy rags" (Isaiah 64:6 KJV).

When Jesus says, "Agree with thine adversary quickly," He does not mean *obey* the devil. He is saying that when Satan accuses you of some sin or flaw, if the devil is even minutely right it is to your advantage to agree with him about your unrighteousness. If he accuses you of being impure or not loving or praying enough, he is right. The key is not to argue with the devil about your own righteousness because, before God, your righteousness *is* unacceptable. No matter how much you defend or justify yourself, you know inwardly that often the accusations of the devil have morsels of truth in them.

Our salvation is not based upon what we do but upon who Jesus becomes to us. Christ Himself is our righteousness. We have been justified by faith; our peace with God comes through our Lord Jesus Christ (see Romans 5:1). When Satan comes against you, he tries to deceive you by focusing your attention upon your own righteousness. The more we recognize that Jesus alone is our righteousness, the less the adversary can assault us in the arena of our failings.

Thus, when the accuser comes seeking to condemn you for not having enough love, your response should be, "That is true, I do not have enough love. But the Son of God died for *all* my sins, even the sin of imperfect love." Step out from the shadow of satanic assault and stand in the brightness of your Father's love. Submit yourself to God and ask for Christ's love and forgiveness to replace your weak and imperfect love.

When Satan seeks to condemn you for impatience, again your response should be, "Yes, in my flesh I am very impatient. But since I have been born again, *Jesus* is my righteousness and through His blood I am forgiven and cleansed." Turn again to God. Use the accusation as a reminder that you are not standing before an angry God but rather a throne of grace which enables you to boldly draw near to God for help (see Hebrews 4:16).

A vital key, therefore, to overcoming the devil is humility. To humble yourself is to refuse to defend your image: *you are corrupt and full of sin in your old nature!* Yet, we have a new nature which has been created in the likeness of Christ (see Ephesians 4:24), so we can agree with our adversary about the condition of our flesh.

But do not limit this principle of humbling yourself only to times of spiritual warfare. This precept is applicable in other situations as well. The strength of humility is that it builds a spiritual defense around your soul, prohibiting strife, competition, and many of life's irritations from stealing your peace.

A wonderful place to practice this is in your family relationships. As a husband, your wife may criticize you for being insensitive. A fleshly response could easily escalate the conversation into a conflict. The alternative is to simply humble yourself and agree with your wife. You probably were insensitive. Then pray together and ask God to give you a more tender love.

As a wife, perhaps your husband accuses you of not understanding the pressures he has at work. More than likely he is right, you do not know the things he must face. Instead of responding with a counter-charge, humble yourself and agree with him. Pray together, asking God to give you an understanding heart. If we remain humble in heart, we will receive abundant grace from God; Satan will be disarmed on many fronts.

Remember, Satan fears virtue. He is terrified of humility; he hates it because humility is the surrender of the soul to the Lord, and the devil is terrified of Jesus Christ.

CHAPTER 3

PULLING DOWN STRONGHOLDS

What men call "salvation" is simply the first stage of God's plan for our lives, which is to conform us in character and power to the image of Jesus Christ. If we fail to see our relationship to God as such, we will allow too many areas within us to remain unchanged. Pulling down strongholds is the demolition and removal of our old ways of thinking so that the actual presence of Jesus Christ can be manifested through us.

WHAT IS A STRONGHOLD?

"For though we walk in the flesh, we do not war according to the flesh. For the weapons of our warfare are not carnal but mighty in God for pulling down strongholds" (2 Corinthians 10:3–4 NKJV).

All successful deliverance must begin by first removing that which defends the enemy. In speaking of spiritual warfare, the apostle Paul enlists the word "stronghold" to define the spiritual fortresses wherein Satan and his legions hide and are protected. These fortresses exist in the thought-patterns and ideas that govern individuals, families, churches, communities and even nations. Before victory can be claimed, these strongholds must be pulled down and Satan's armor removed. Then the mighty weapons of the Word and the Spirit can effectively plunder Satan's house.

But what is the biblical meaning of this word, *stronghold*. In the Old Testament, a stronghold was a fortified dwelling used as a means of protection from an enemy. We find that David hid from King Saul in wilderness strongholds at Horesh (see 1 Samuel 23:14,19). These were physical structures, usually caves high on a mountainside, and were very difficult to assault. It was with this imagery in mind that the inspired writers of the Bible adapted the word *stronghold* to define powerful, vigorously protected spiritual realities.

A stronghold can be a source of protection for us from the devil, as is the case when the Lord becomes our stronghold (see Psalm 18:2). Or conversely, a stronghold can be a source of defense for the devil, where demonic or sinful activity is actually defended within us by our sympathetic thoughts toward evil. The strongholds we are going to expose first are those wrong attitudes that protect and defend the old self-life, which very often become the fortified dwellings of demonic oppression in a person's life.

The apostle Paul defines a stronghold as "speculations, . . . [a] lofty thing raised up against the knowledge of God" (2 Corinthians 10:5). A demonic stronghold is any type of thinking that exalts itself above the knowledge of God, thereby giving the devil a secure place of influence in an individual's thought-life.

In most cases, we are not talking about demonic possession. This author does not believe that a Christian can be possessed, for *possession* implies ownership. If one has given his life to Christ, he has become the property of the Son of God and is, in truth, purchased by Christ.

However, Christians can be *oppressed* by demons, which can occupy unregenerated thought-systems, especially if those thoughts are defended by self-deception or false doctrines. The thought, "I cannot have a demon because I am a Christian," is simply untrue. A demon cannot have you in an eternal, possessive sense, but you can have a demon if you refuse to repent of your sympathetic thoughts toward evil. Your rebellion toward God provides a place for the devil in your life.

A number of Christians are tormented by various fears. They have been counseled and prayed over but to little avail. They needed more than prayer; they needed deliverance. But deliverance will probably be far from them until the spirit of fear is confronted and bound, and the stronghold of fear cast down.

Many believers have been taught that, because they have the Holy Spirit, they cannot be deceived. This also is untrue. One reason the Spirit of Truth was sent was because we so easily fall into self-deception. In fact, the very thought that a Christian cannot be deceived is itself a deception! Once a particular lie permeates a believer's mind, his ideas and opinions crystallize and remain in whatever state of spiritual immaturity he happens to be. All manner of spirits will attack the soul, knowing they are protected by the armor of that person's own thoughts and doctrines.

It is quite difficult to break the power of religious self-deception, for the very nature of faith is to give no room for doubt. Once a person is deceived, he does not recognize that he is deceived, because he has been deceived! For all that we think we know, we must know this as well: we can be wrong. If we refuse to accept this truth, how will we ever be corrected from our errors?

Any area of our heart or mind that is not surrendered to Jesus Christ is an area vulnerable to satanic attack. And it is here, uniquely in the uncrucified thought-life of the believer's mind, that the pulling down of strongholds is of vital importance. For this reason, we must attain what the Scriptures call "humility of mind" before real deliverance is possible. When we discover rebellion toward God within us, we must not defend or excuse ourselves. Rather, we must humble our hearts and repent, exercising our faith in God to change us.

You see, Satan feeds upon sin. Wherever there is a habit of sin in a believer's life, expect to find demonic activity in that area. The sin-habit often becomes the dwelling place for a spirit that is robbing a believer of power and joy, and that habitation (or habit) is a stronghold.

You may not agree with the idea that evil spirits can frequent and occupy attitudes in a believer's life, but you must certainly agree that each of us has a carnal mind which is a source of vain imaginations and thoughts that exalt themselves above God (see 2 Corinthians 10:3–5). We deal with the devil by dealing with the carnal thought-systems, the strongholds, that protect the enemy.

There were no strongholds, no wrong attitudes, no faulty thinking processes in Christ's mind. Just before Jesus went to His death, He remarked, "The ruler of the world is coming, and he has nothing in Me" (John 14:30). Satan had nothing in Jesus.

We also want to be able to say that Satan has no secret area inside us, no temptation he can stage that will open the door of our soul toward evil. When the strongholds of our minds are toppled, though we may still occasionally fall into sin, we will walk in great victory. And we will be instrumental in helping others in their deliverance as well.

REPENTANCE PRECEDES DELIVERANCE

The pulling down of strongholds begins with repentance. When Jesus sent out His disciples, "They went out and preached that men should repent. And they were casting out many demons and were anointing with oil many sick people and healing them" (Mark 6:12–13). Note the sequence of recovery: they called men to repent, then they delivered them of demons, then consecrated them with oil and healed them. *Repentance precedes deliverance, and deliverance often leads to healing in other areas.*

If you have been a Christian for any length of time, you have already had many strongholds broken in your life. These were broken when you repented and came to Jesus. Deliverance is often just that simple when a soul is willing. Yet, without some measure of repentance, deliverance is almost always impossible, for although a spirit may be commanded to leave, if the structure of the individual's thoughts has not been changed, his wrong attitude toward sin will welcome that spirit back.

One aspect of Christ's ministry is that "thoughts from many hearts may be revealed" (Luke 2:35). If you are truly walking with Jesus, many areas of your thinking processes will be exposed. Yet, there will be a power from God to enable you to repent and receive His virtue into your life. You will see strongholds fall and victory come. But I must warn you, there will be pressure from your flesh, as well as from the demonic world itself, to minimize or ignore what God is requiring of you in your repentance. You may be tempted to surrender just a token sin or some minor fault, while allowing your most serious iniquity to remain entrenched and well-hidden. Let us realize, therefore, that *the energies we expend in keeping our sins secret are the actual "materials" of which a stronghold is made. The demon you are fighting is actually using your thoughts to protect his access to your life.*

Let's pray: *Heavenly Father, there are areas in my life (audibly name the habitual sins) that I have not fully surrendered to my Lord, Jesus Christ. Lord, forgive me of compromise. I also ask You for courage to approach the pulling down of strongholds without reluctance or willful deception in my heart.*

By the power of the Holy Spirit and in the name of Jesus, I bind the satanic influences that were reinforcing compromise and sin within me. I submit myself to the light of the Spirit of Truth to expose the strongholds of sin within me.

By the mighty weapons of the Spirit and the Word, I proclaim that each stronghold in my life is coming down! I purpose, by the grace of God, to have only one stronghold within me: the stronghold of the presence of Christ!

I thank You, Lord, for forgiving and cleansing me from all my sins. And by the grace of God, I commit myself to follow through in this area until even the ruins of this stronghold are removed from my mind! Thank You, Father. In Jesus' name. Amen.

CHAPTER 4

A HOUSE
MADE OF THOUGHTS

There are satanic strongholds over countries and communities and there are strongholds which influence churches and individuals. Wherever a stronghold exists, it is a demonically induced pattern of thinking. Specifically, it is a "house made of thoughts" which has become a dwelling place for satanic activity.

A WARNING BEFORE DELIVERANCE!

"Now when the unclean spirit goes out of a man, it passes through waterless places, seeking rest, and does not find it. Then it says, 'I will return to my house from which I came' " (Matthew 12:43–44).

Although the nature of an unclean spirit is, by definition, spiritual and not physical, it still seeks a dwelling place, a "house" where it may "rest." Jesus revealed that there is a dimension to human nature that actually can host an evil spirit and provide it a type of rest. If that is so, let us expose the nature of man and uncover that aspect in us which can become the "construction material" within which a spirit might lodge.

First let us realize that a demon cannot dwell in a true Christian's spirit. Through regeneration, the human spirit becomes the home of the Holy Spirit. Indeed, it is because the Holy Spirit is within us that we have discernment concerning the enemy's inroads.

The dimension of the human soul which is most similar in disposition to the demonic realm is our carnal nature. It is uniquely in our uncrucified thoughts and unsanctified attitudes that unclean spirits, masking themselves as our thoughts and hiding themselves in our attitudes, find access into our lives.

Thus, to secure deliverance, Jesus explained, "When [the unclean spirit] comes, it finds [its house] unoccupied, swept, and put in order. Then it goes, and takes along with it seven other spirits more wicked than itself, and they go in and live there; and the last state of that man becomes worse than the first" (Matthew 12:44–45).

If we are going to be successful in spiritual battle, we must seek more than just relief from our enemy; we must pursue conformity to Christ. Thus, for deliverance to bear fruit, the nature of Christ must be assimilated into the delivered soul. Otherwise, there is the danger that the "last state of that man" might become "worse than the first" (Matthew 12:45; 2 Peter 2:20). Our quest is to seek to establish the righteousness of Christ in the very area of our hearts where Satan once dwelt. Except in cases of physical affliction or mental torment, we should not attempt deliverance for anyone unwilling to repent and submit their thought-life to Jesus Christ.

REMOVING SATAN'S ARMOR

When a strong man, fully armed, guards his own house, his possessions are undisturbed. But when someone stronger than he attacks him and overpowers him, he takes away from him all his armor on which he had relied and distributes his plunder.   —Luke 11:21–22

Before we were saved, you and I were "undisturbed" possessions of the devil; Satan was like a fully armed "strong man" guarding the homestead of our souls. On the day of our salvation, however, "someone stronger," the Lord Jesus Christ, attacked and overpowered Satan and stripped him of his armor. Our born-again experiences may be widely varied on a natural level, but in the spirit-realm, a very similar war was waged and won for each of us. If we could have seen into the invisible world, we would have observed the Holy Spirit working with the angels of God to destroy the enemy's first line of defense, his "armor." What exactly was this armor that protected the devil and kept us from salvation? The armor upon which demons rely consists of our own thoughts, attitudes and opinions which are in agreement with evil.

What Jesus described as "armor," the apostle Paul classified as "strongholds" (2 Corinthians 10:1–4 NKJV). It is important to recognize that, in speaking of strongholds, the apostle is addressing the church! It is foolish to assume that our salvation experience has eliminated all the wrong ideas and attitudes—the strongholds—that are still influencing our perceptions and behavior. Yes, old things passed away and truly new things have come but, until we are walking in the fullness of Christ, we should not assume that the process of change is over.

We will be identifying some of these strongholds later in this chapter. For now, let us say that, on an individual level, the foundation of our continued success in warfare comes from yielding to the Lord as He reveals these strongholds and agreeing with Him through repentance in pulling them down.

It is important to recognize that when we speak of strongholds we are not talking about random thoughts or occasional sins. Rather, the strongholds that affect us most are those which are so hidden in our thinking patterns that we do not recognize them nor identify them as evil. Remember, in our initial text, Jesus revealed that unclean spirits are seeking "rest." The sense of rest they seek originates from being in harmony with their environment. In other words, when our thought-life is in agreement with unbelief, fear or habitual sin, the enemy has rest.

It is significant that the process of deliverance quite often involves a season of inner conflict and turmoil. This is a good sign, signifying the individual's will desires to be free. We should expect a time where we must exercise our authority in Christ as we "resist" the devil (1 Peter 5:8–9). Paul speaks of the "struggle" of the church against principalities and powers (Ephesians 6:12). There will be a period of fighting involved in the process of pulling down strongholds, for you are breaking your agreement with a foe who will fight to remain in your life.

TAKING EVERY THOUGHT CAPTIVE TO CHRIST

While we may find comfort in being Christians, being a Christian has not made us perfect. There are still many strongholds within us. Therefore, let us identify some of these spiritual fortresses. Rare is the Christian who is not limited by at least one of the following strongholds: unbelief, cold love, fear, pride, unforgiveness, lust, greed, or any combination of these, as well as the possibility of many others.

Because we excuse ourselves so readily, it is difficult to discern the areas of oppression in our lives. After all, these are *our* thoughts, attitudes and perceptions; we justify and defend our thoughts with the same degree of intensity with which we justify and defend ourselves. As it is written, "As [a man] thinketh in his heart, so is he" (Proverbs 23:7 KJV). In other words, the essence of who we are exists in our thought-life. Therefore, before any deliverance can truly be accomplished, we must honestly recognize and confess our need. We must stop pretending everything is all right. We must humble ourselves and seek help. Indeed, as previously mentioned, the first stronghold that God must remove is pride. For until one is willing to admit that he needs deliverance, he will never be free from strongholds.

In order to recognize what is wrong in us, we must perceive God's standard of right. David in the height of ecstasy and Job in the pit of misery, as well as all who have pondered life, faced the same question: What is man? The writer of Hebrews also asks this question, but the answer he receives lifts us up to see the face of God, and "We . . . see . . . Jesus" (Hebrews 2:9). From the Father's view, *the mystery of man's identity is unveiled in the life of Jesus Christ.* Christ is the "firstborn among many brethren" (Romans 8:29). He is first born of a heavenly genesis; He is the Father's plan for mankind. When we consider the mystery of humanity, we find our answer in beholding Jesus Christ. He is not only our Savior, He is also the indwelling One who conforms us to Himself (Hebrews 2:10; Romans 8:28–29).

Let us also realize that only Jesus can be Jesus. As we yield to Him in increasing degrees of surrender, as we abide in Him and His Word abides in us, He brings forth life that is not simply like His own, but is His very life! Christ Himself living within us fulfills God's eternal purpose, which is to make man in His image. It is the presence of the Lord Jesus coming forth in us that makes the weapons of our warfare mighty, empowering our words with authority as we pull down strongholds.

Therefore, you must learn to look objectively at any thoughts or attitudes that fail to conform to the likeness and teachings of Jesus. Those thoughts must be captured and wrong attitudes crucified. We must make way in us for the coming of the Lord. We must allow the increase of His presence to be so absorbed into our spirits that we not only believe in Him, we believe *like* Him. His love, thoughts and desires flow out from within us as naturally as fruit from a vine.

Consequently, when we seek to identify and destroy demonic strongholds, the second fortress that must be annihilated is the stronghold of unbelief. It is this scheme of thinking, which tells us attaining Christlikeness is impossible, that holds all further spiritual growth hostage. This lie and the chains it places upon our hearts must be broken from our lives, for Christlikeness is not only possible, it is our destiny.

Accordingly, let us take this moment to pray. Let the Holy Spirit rise and flood your heart. If you suffer from the stronghold of unbelief which says you will never be like Christ, that deception can begin to break right now.

Let us pray: *Lord Jesus, I submit to You. I declare, according to the Word of God, that because of Your power to subject all things unto Yourself, the weapons of my warfare are mighty to the pulling down of strongholds (2 Corinthians 10:3–4). I repent for using the lie, "I will never be like Jesus," as an excuse to sin and compromise my convictions. In Jesus' name, I renounce my flawed, sinful old nature and by the grace of God and the power of Your Spirit I pull down the stronghold of unbelief that exists in my mind. Because of the perfect sacrifice of Jesus Christ, I am a new creation. And I believe that I will go from glory to glory, being continually transformed into Christ's image as I walk with Him in His grace.*

DEFEAT THE STRONGHOLD OF FAILURE!

Let us look at other strongholds that may be in your life and see their origin and, more importantly, how they can be removed. First, remember that a stronghold is a house made of thoughts. Therefore, in regard to this type of warfare, Paul explained that our success is based upon "taking every thought captive to the obedience of Christ" (2 Corinthians 10:5). Since our goal is to allow the Spirit of Christ full access into our souls, we must capture our thoughts and make them slaves to Christ.

To deal with the stronghold of failure, we must make repentance our way of life. Bear in mind also that *repentance* means "change," not merely remorse. Our thinking must change. There are herds of erroneous thoughts roaming across our minds, grazing upon the ever-available hay and stubble of unbelief and failure. Thoughts like "I will always be a failure" or "I am just a sinner" or "I tried walking in the Spirit but it didn't work" converge and form the walls, floor and ceiling—the building material of the stronghold of failure. To secure victory, you must capture these wrong thoughts.

Capture the thought, "I am a failure!" Repent of it, asking the Lord to forgive you of your unbelief. Let your mind be renewed by the Word of God which states, "I can do all things through Him who strengthens me" (Philippians 4:13). Even though you have failed and will fail again in the future, now because Christ is in your life you can confidently proclaim, "Though I was a failure, my sufficiency comes from God, not myself. He causes all things to work for my good so that nothing is impossible if I keep faith in Him."

Arrest the thought, "I am just a sinner!" Replace it with the confession of your faith which says, "Though I was a sinner, now I am a beloved child of God and, though I occasionally still sin, the blood of Christ cleanses me of all unrighteousness" (see 1 John 1:7–9). Because of the blood, Christ's sacrifice makes each of us pure "just as He is pure" (1 John 3:3). By capturing your self-condemning thoughts and identifying yourself as God's child, you are tearing down a stronghold of defeat that once oppressed you. In its place you are building a godly stronghold of faith, which is built upon the Word of God. With the old stronghold exposed and the thought-patterns of defeatism coming down, the Word of God will begin to renew you in the spirit of your mind. You will need to persevere in your victory, but as you do, you will begin to walk in tremendous power and peace. You will enter the godly stronghold of faith.

Let it be established in your attitudes that the goal and purpose of your salvation is that you be conformed to the likeness of Christ. Is it not written, "Whom He foreknew, He also predestined to become conformed to the image of His Son" (Romans 8:29)? The same Lord who conquered the devil and liberated your heart in salvation is working still to renew your mind. While it is true that He is our promised land, it is also true that we are His promised land! The giants within our hearts, though they have withstood and humbled us, shall not withstand Him! He is the eternal Lord of Hosts, the Holy One who knows no defeat!

As long as we recognize that our salvation is a continual transformation, and that we are changing from "glory to glory"

(2 Corinthians 3:18) into the image of Christ, we should not be discouraged by the strongholds we discover; nor will occasional or momentary setbacks render us impotent. As we see our need, we rejoice in knowing it is only a matter of time before another giant is removed!

DESTROYING THE STRONGHOLD OF FEAR!

Another stronghold that oppresses men is fear. Your experience tells you that if you try something new, especially in front of people, you may be embarrassed and rejected. To counter this, a whole series of reactions emerges in your mind. You sit back when you should step forward. You are silent when you should be speaking. That silent, fearful withdrawal into yourself has become a house made of thoughts, wherein dwells a spirit of fear.

God does not want us in bondage. He has not given us a "spirit of fear," but of love, power and a sound mind (2 Timothy 1:7 KJV). Therefore, let us look at some of the thoughts and experiences that may have formed the structure of this tormenting fortress of fear. Perhaps, when you attempted something new as a young child, the reaction among your family or friends was ridicule. Their thoughtless words went so deep that, in recoiling from the pain, you have involuntarily remained in the recoiled or withdrawn position. Since then, you have refused to place yourself in situations where you can become vulnerable to criticism. You may not even remember the incident(s), but you have not stopped recoiling even until today.

Remember, Jesus said the Father would forgive us as we forgave others. As unjust as it may seem, your *reaction* to what hurt you was as detrimental to your well-being as were the original, offending words. In fact, your reaction has actually become a part of your nature. You can be delivered from that oppression on your soul by releasing and forgiving those who hurt you. To the degree that you truly let the incident go and forgive the offender, to that same degree God will restore your soul to a balanced and healthy attitude toward people. As you increase in this process of forgiveness, you will grow in love and, as the Scripture says, "There is no fear in love . . . love casts out fear" (1 John 4:18). The stronghold of fear will be replaced by the stronghold of love.

Let's pray now against the stronghold of fear:

Blessed Lord, You are my Redeemer and King. What can man do to me? I repent for accommodating mistrust, fear and insecurity. I release those who have wounded me in the past and I step into the stronghold of Your loving protection. I speak to the spirit of fear—it has no place in my life. In Jesus' name. Amen!

Always remember: Victory begins with the name of Jesus on our lips, but it will not be consummated until the nature of Jesus is in our hearts. It is not enough to have your "house . . . swept, and put in order" (Matthew 12:44); your thought-life must be occupied by the person of Christ. As you persist in yielding yourself to Christ, He will remove Satan's armor from your mind. He will show you what you need to bring down. You will see that the weapons of your warfare are mighty to the pulling down of strongholds!

CHAPTER 5

THREE SOURCES
OF STRONGHOLDS

*If you want to identify the hidden strongholds in your life,
you need only survey the attitudes in your heart. Every area
in your thinking that glistens with hope in God is an area that
is being liberated by Christ. But any system of thinking that
does not have hope, which feels hopeless, is a stronghold that
must be pulled down.*

THE FIRST SOURCE OF STRONGHOLDS:
THE WORLD

Generally speaking, strongholds originate from any one of
three sources. The first is the very world into which we have
been born. Perhaps the greatest source of strongholds found in
our hearts comes from the steady stream of information and
experiences that continually shaped our childhood perceptions.

The amount of love (or lack of love) in our home, our cultural environment, peer values and pressures, as well as fears of rejection and exposure—even our physical appearance and intelligence—all combine to form our sense of identity and our view of life.

Our souls, wrought with insecurities, are highly sensitive to the criticisms and compliments of others. Such words are poured into young hearts like molten steel which, as they cool, are fused into our natures. How many of today's adults believe they are mentally slow simply because, as children, they absorbed into their self-concept the thoughtless scolding of a teacher or parent?

These concepts and limitations are structured into us from childhood, built into our thinking patterns through the words, ideas and examples of others. *Indeed, many of our opinions about life are ours only because we know of no other way to think.* Yet, we defend and protect our ideas, justifying our opinions as though they were ours alone, born in the very womb of our own creativity!

Another example of strongholds created by the world occurs when Christians accept as true the falsehood of astrology. Though most Christians would confess that astrology is false, in their inner man they accept the characteristics of their zodiac sign as basically true. In their search for identity, this mixture of generalization and illusions was absorbed into their soul where it continues to stand even today, persistently whispering words of opposition to God's work of transformation.

As Christians, only the truth of Jesus Christ qualifies us to enter eternal life. He must be our primary mentor and ultimate instructor; otherwise, we will simply conform to the limitations and patterns of our worldly teachers, and we will never rise higher than the standards of our culture. Our teachers and fathers more than likely did the best they could. Yet, our goal is not simply to do the deeds of our fathers but to do the deeds of Jesus.

Therefore, Scripture instructs us to consider the outcome of a man's way of life before we submit to his religious concepts (see Hebrews 13:7). Of course, the Lord will certainly use people to teach and equip us, yet we must have higher goals than becoming followers of men. Our goal must be conformity to Jesus Christ. Yes, we follow godly leaders, but we are following those who are following Christ (see 1 Corinthians 11:1; Philippians 3:17). Only Jesus, by His resurrection, proved He knew the deep mysteries surrounding mankind; by conquering death He demonstrated He understood life.

You see, when we come to Christ, all that we are in nature and character is destined to change. The Bible tells us God has provided for us a new heart, a new mind, a new spirit, a new nature and, ultimately, even a new name! (see Ezekiel 36:26; Hebrews 8:10; 1 Corinthians 2:16; 2 Corinthians 5:16–17; Revelation 2:17)

When you were born again you received the very Spirit of God, and through His Spirit you were birthed into another realm: the kingdom of heaven. Though your feet are still on earth, through the vehicle of the Holy Spirit you are united to the actual person of Jesus Christ, who is seated at the throne of God. Even as your limbs are attached to your torso, so your heart is attached to the power of God. You are never alone. Christ is always with you. What you were as a person prior to salvation, you will never be again!

The promise of God is this: "If any one is in Christ, he is a new creature; the old things passed away; behold, new things have come" (2 Corinthians 5:17). Everything, even your intelligence and physical appearance, is now subject to change for the better. This is why our culture and the boundaries of worldly knowledge must not be allowed to rule over us, for old limitations are destined to go. New faith and hope should be growing within you daily.

How do we attain such a wonderful new beginning? We receive the Spirit of Christ into our hearts to empower us. We study the words of Christ to direct us. And whatever we find in us that is not like Jesus, we crucify.

THE STRONGHOLD OF OUR EXPERIENCES

Another means through which strongholds are structured into our souls is through our experiences and the often erroneous conclusions we draw from them. Our firsthand knowledge, for better or worse, becomes the substructure of what we define as reality. Yet, our experiences, while perfectly valid, are not necessarily conclusive. Unless they actually have become a fulfillment of God's Word, we must consider our experiences incomplete. We must not allow what we have experienced to diminish our trust in God.

Consider: Abraham lived for 25 years as an old man trusting that God would give him a son. For a quarter of a century, Abraham tried to have a child, yet he experienced only failure. Sarah could not become pregnant. If Abraham had allowed his subjective experience to guide him, he would not have become the father of our faith. Yet, in spite of his subjective experience, he continued to believe God. We read, "With respect to the promise of God, [Abraham] did not waver in unbelief but grew strong in faith, giving glory to God, and being fully assured that what God had promised, He was able also to perform" (Romans 4:20–21).

Abraham's experience was valid in that he and Sarah were, indeed, incapable of producing offspring. Yet, *Abraham did not allow his experience to decrease his faith.* Rather, he "grew strong in faith, giving glory to God." This is the nature of faith, and faith must triumph over experiences until experiences conform to the Word of God.

You see, everyone who has a promise from God will pass through situations that seem to be the exact opposite of what they expected. At some point, we will be required to look our experience of failure or delay or impotency in the face, yet believe God anyway. As the Scripture declares: "Let God be found true, though every man be found a liar" (Romans 3:4).

We may value our experiences, but what must rule our hearts is the Word of God. In other words, even though we were not healed, we should not conclude that healing is not for today. God's provision is eternal, which means that until heaven and earth pass away, He has provided for all our needs. In regard to sin, though we might repeatedly stumble, we must continue to believe God for grace to overcome. We must give ourselves room to grow into new insights. We must never surrender our faith in God's Word! If the conclusions we draw from our experiences leave us thinking that Jesus is not the same today as He was in the Gospels, the conclusion we have drawn is wrong. It is a stronghold that must be pulled down.

THE STRONGHOLD OF WRONG DOCTRINES

A third source of strongholds comes from false church doctrines and teachings. Jesus warned, "See to it that no one misleads you" (Matthew 24:4). We can be led by another person, but we must take responsibility that we are not misled by that individual. We must study and know the Bible ourselves. If we do not, how can we discern if there is error in the teachings we hear? As much as we love a particular pastor, as often as we have been edified by him, we must humbly ask the Lord to confirm any questionable doctrines. No teacher is so true, no ministry so pure that we can blindly let them lead us. They may lead us, but our eyes must be open and our ears sensitive to the confirming voice of the Holy Spirit. As it is written, "Every fact is to be confirmed by the testimony of two or three witnesses" (2 Corinthians 13:1). Even true teachers can innocently communicate false doctrines. It does not matter how sincere our Bible teachers are. If the preponderance of what they are teaching does not lead us into greater surrender to Christ's love, holiness and power, their theology can actually become a stronghold that will limit us and oppress our spiritual growth.

The safest way to insure that no one misleads us is to see to it we do not mislead ourselves. We must stay honest with God and sensitive to His love and His Word. Satan's plan is to make us somehow accept, either through our upbringing, our experiences or through false church dogma, that certain portions of the life of Christ are untrue or not valid in our case. Every battle we face in life is over the Word and whether or not we can build our lives upon the faithfulness and integrity of God. If we hold fast to those things of which we are sure, God will be faithful to deliver us from every stronghold and lead us fully into His kingdom.

CHAPTER 6

THE STRONGHOLD OF CHRIST'S LIKENESS

Victory begins with the name of Jesus on our lips. It is consummated by the nature of Jesus in our hearts.

GOD'S HIGHEST PURPOSE

Most Christians only engage in spiritual warfare with a hope of either relieving present distresses or attaining a "normal" existence. However, the purpose of all aspects of spirituality, warfare included, is to bring us into the image of Christ. Nothing, not worship nor warfare, neither love nor deliverance, is truly attainable if we miss the singular objective of our faith: Christlikeness.

Let us recall that the Lord delivered the ancient Hebrews out of Egypt so He could bring them into the Promised Land. Likewise, we are delivered out of sin, not that we might live for ourselves, but that we might come into Christlikeness. Our goals must align with God's, for if our nature does not change we will invariably find ourselves entangled in the same problems that caused our difficulties in the first place.

While we may not want to hear this, many of our spiritual conflicts simply are not going to cease until the character of the Lord Jesus is formed in our hearts. The Father's goal in deliverance is much more than simply seeing our burdens or the devil taken off our backs. Indeed, the specific purpose toward which God steers the working of all things in our lives is our conformity "to the image of His Son." The Father's purpose in our salvation was that Jesus would become "the firstborn among many brethren" (Romans 8:29). In other words, the way to realize God's ultimate victory is to reach toward His ultimate goal, which is complete transformation into the likeness of Christ.

There is an interpenetration of spirit between God and ourselves where our spirits are fully saturated with the living presence of the Lord Jesus, where His glory so floods our lives that there is "no dark part" left within us (Luke 11:36). This immediacy of the Lord's presence produces an indestructible defense, a fortress within which we are hidden from evil. Through Him, we enter the excellence of His ways in our relationships both with the Father and one another, thereby walking in immunity from countless satanic attacks. Indeed, as His fullness within us increases, that which is written is fulfilled: "As He is, so also are we in this world" and "He who was born of God keeps [us] and the evil one does not touch [us]" (1 John 4:17; 1 John 5:18).

We must realize that it is not Satan who defeats us; it is our openness to him. To perfectly subdue the devil we must walk in the "shelter of the Most High" (Psalm 91:1). Satan is tolerated for one purpose: the warfare between the devil and God's saints thrusts us into Christlikeness, where the nature of Christ becomes our only place of rest and security. God allows warfare to facilitate His eternal plan, which is to make man in His image (see Genesis 1:26).

Once we realize that the Father's goal is to transform our lives, we will continually find that God has one answer to spiritual warfare: *appropriate the nature of His Son!* Are you troubled by demons of fear or doubt? Submit *those* areas to God, repenting of your unbelief, and then yield yourself to Christ's faith within you. Are you troubled with spirits of lust and shame? Present those very areas of sin to God, repenting of your old nature, drawing upon the forgiveness of Christ and His purity of heart.

The Father is more concerned with the coming forth of His Son in our lives than He is in defeating Satan. Who is the devil, that he can defy the living God? Indeed, it is of the greatest truth that once the devil recognizes his assault against your life has not pulled you from God but toward Him—once he perceives that his temptations are actually forcing you to appropriate the virtue of Christ—the enemy will withdraw.

THE GOAL IS CHRISTLIKENESS, NOT WARFARE

There is a time, which we will speak of later in this book, when the Lord will lead us to confront the strongholds of hell over our churches and our communities. There is another time, however, when to engage in much spiritual warfare is actually a distraction from your obedience to God. Jesus defeated Satan in Gethsemane and at the cross, not by directly confronting the devil but by fulfilling the destiny to which He had been called at Calvary. *The greatest battle that was ever won was accom-*

plished by the apparent death of the victor, without even a word of rebuke to His adversary. The prince of this world was judged and principalities and powers were disarmed not by confrontational warfare but by the surrender of Jesus Christ on the cross.

There are occasions when your battle against the devil is actually a digression from the higher purpose God has for you. Intercessors and warfare leaders take note: there is a demon whose purpose is to lure one's mind into hell. If we were to name this spirit, we would call it "Wrong Focus." You may be fighting this very spirit if you are continually seeing evil spirits in people or in the material world around you. The ultimate goal of this demon is to produce mental illness in saints who move in deliverance. Listen very carefully: we are not called to focus on the battle or the devil, except when that battle hinders our immediate transformation into Christ's likeness. *Our calling is to focus on Jesus.* The work of the devil, however, is to draw our eyes from Jesus. Satan's first weapon always involves luring our eyes from Christ. Turn toward Jesus and almost immediately the battle vanishes.

I knew a man once who owned a record company. Besides running the operation, he also spent many hours in production listening to the "mother disk," which was the master from which all subsequent recordings were produced. Over the years, his ears became adept at catching the "pops and sizzles," the imperfections that had to be eliminated in the master. I remarked one day that I thought working with music must be enjoyable. His response was enlightening. He said, "You know, I haven't listened to music in years. When I turn on my sophisticated home stereo, no matter what recording I'm listening to, all I hear are the pops and sizzles."

In the same way his thoughts were bent toward musical imperfections, so Wrong Focus will seek to turn your thoughts continually toward the enemy. Suddenly, all you will see are demons. The true gift called "discerning of spirits" is a balanced gift which enables you to recognize at least as many angelic spirits as you do evil spirits. The proper manifestation of this gift has a much more positive focus and influence than what commonly masquerades as discernment.

An example of the proper balance in discernment is seen in 2 Kings. The Syrian army had surrounded Dothan, a city in Israel, much to the consternation of the prophet Elisha's servant. To calm his attendant's fright, Elisha prayed that his servant's eyes would be opened. He then encouraged his servant, saying, "Do not fear, for those who are with us are more than those who are with them" (2 Kings 6:16). As the Lord opened the servant's eyes, he saw what Elisha saw: "The mountain was full of horses and chariots of fire all around Elisha" (v. 17).

In spiritual warfare, the battle is never limited to an "us against them" human affair. It always includes "those . . . with us" against "those . . . with them." True discernment is as fully aware of the vast multitude of angels loyal to God as it is aware of the activity of the demonic realm—and it is aware that the angelic hosts on our side are both stronger and more numerous than the enemy. Remember, if you fail to "hear the music" in your times of warfare, your discernment is incomplete.

We must learn that, on a personal level, it is better to develop godly virtues than to spend our day praying against the devil. Indeed, it is the joy of the Lord that casts out spirits of depression. It is our living faith which destroys spirits of unbelief; it is aggressive love which casts out fear.

As we continually yield ourselves to Christ, surrendering ourselves by faith to His nature and His words, we literally

CHAPTER **7**

RULE IN THE MIDST OF YOUR ENEMIES!

True peace does not come from extreme indifference, nor does it originate from becoming so "spiritual" that you fail to notice the world around you. Peace is the fruit of being confident in God's love; it is born of the revelation that, regardless of the battle, "Greater is He who is in you than he who is in the world" (1 John 4:4). You are not self-assured, you are God-assured.

THE GOD OF PEACE WILL CRUSH SATAN

To wage effective spiritual warfare, we must understand and use spiritual authority. Spiritual authority, however, is not forcing your will upon another person. When you have spiritual authority, you have established God's peace in an area that once was full of conflict and oppression. Therefore, to truly be able to move in authority, we must first have peace.

The apostle Paul taught, "The God of peace will soon crush Satan under your feet" (Romans 16:20). When we maintain peace during warfare, it is a crushing deathblow to satanic oppression and fear. Our victory never comes from our emotions or our intellect. Our victory comes by refusing to judge by what our eyes see or our ears hear and by trusting that what God has promised will come to pass.

We will never know Christ's victory in its fullness until we stop reacting humanly to our circumstances. When you truly have authority over something you can look at that thing without worry, fear or intimidation. *Your peace is the proof of your victory.* Jesus' authority over the violent storm (see Matthew 8:23–27) was the exercise and expansion of His peace over the elements. He did not fight against the storm, nor did He fear it. He faced its fury and subdued it with His authority, in perfect peace. In Pilate's court, in a world stirred to an emotional frenzy by the powers of hell, a holy tranquility surrounded Christ—peace that was born out of His resolve to do God's will no matter what the cost. His Spirit emanated a calm that perfectly represented the peace at God's throne. In a matter of moments it was no longer Jesus who was on trial, but Satan, Pilate and the religious establishment in Israel.

Satan's arsenal consists of such things as fear, worry, doubt and self-pity. Every one of these weapons robs us of peace and leaves us troubled inside. Do you want to discern where the enemy is coming against you? In the network of your relationships, wherever you do not have peace, you have war. Conversely, wherever you have peace, you have victory. When Satan hurls his darts against you, the more peace you have during adversity, the more truly you are walking in Christ's victory.

Paul tells us to be "in no way alarmed by your opponents—which is a sign of destruction for them, but of salvation for you" (Philippians 1:28). Your peace, your immovable stand upon the Word of God is a sign that you are positioned correctly in focused submission to the will of God. The very fact that you are "in no way alarmed" by your adversary is a sign that you have authority over him.

PEACEMAKERS ARE SONS OF GOD

Peace is spirit power. Peace is an attribute of the Holy Spirit, and when you are walking in peace, you are walking in power. A peacemaker is not merely someone who protests against war; he is one who is inwardly so yielded to Christ in spirit and purpose that he can be called a son of God (see Matthew 5:9). Where he goes, God goes and where God goes, he goes. He is fearless, calm and bold. Peace emanates from him the way light and heat radiate from fire.

In the battles of life, your peace is actually a weapon. Indeed, your confidence declares that you are not falling for the lies of the devil. You see, the first step toward having spiritual authority over the adversary is having peace in spite of our circumstances. When Jesus confronted the devil, He did not confront Satan with His emotions or in fear. Knowing that the devil was a liar, He simply refused to be influenced by any other voice than God's. His peace overwhelmed Satan. His authority then shattered the lie, which sent demons fleeing.

REST BEFORE RULE

In the 23rd Psalm, David declared, "Even though I walk through the valley of the shadow of death, I fear no evil, for You are with me" (v. 4). There is a place of walking with God where you simply "fear no evil." During his lifetime, David faced many enemies, including a lion, a bear and a giant. In this psalm he stood in the "shadow of death" itself, yet he feared no evil. David's trust was in the Lord. He said, "You are with me." Because God is with you, every adversity you face will unfold in victory as you maintain your faith in God. David continued, "You prepare a table before me in the presence of my enemies" (v. 5). The battle you are in will soon become a meal to you, an experience that will nourish and build you up spiritually.

Only God's peace will quell your fleshly reactions in battle. The source of God's peace is God Himself. Indeed, "Before the throne there was something like a sea of glass, like crystal" (Revelation 4:6). The glass sea is a symbol: there are no ripples, no waves, no anxieties troubling God. The Lord is never worried, never in a hurry nor without an answer. The sea around Him is perfectly still and totally calm. All our victories flow out from being seated here with Him.

God is our Father. The heavenly Jerusalem is our mother, the birthplace of our new nature (see Galatians 4:26). And you, you are a beloved child of God, part of the Father's family and a member of His household (see Ephesians 2:19). You must know by revelation that you are not struggling to get into heaven; rather, you were born there in spiritual rebirth (see John 3:1–8 AMP). Let your heart be settled and positioned correctly in your relationship with the Almighty.

To those who have been born again from above, He says, "Sit at My right hand until I make Your enemies a footstool for

Your feet" (Psalm 110:1). Before you go into warfare, recognize that it is not you that the devil is afraid of; it is Christ in you! We have been raised up and seated with Christ in heavenly places (see Ephesians 2:6). This is why the Holy Spirit continues to speak to us that worship of God is our first response in battle. Position yourself in the presence of God. Sit, at rest, in the knowledge that Christ has already made your enemies the footstool for your feet. From a position of rest, the Word of the Lord continues, "The Lord will stretch forth Your strong scepter from Zion, saying, 'Rule in the midst of Your enemies' " (Psalm 110:2).

Rest precedes rule. Peace precedes power. Do not seek to rule over the devil until you are submitting to God's rule over you. The focal point of all victory comes from seeking God until you find Him, and having found Him, allowing His presence to fill your spirit with His peace. From full assurance at His right hand, as you rest in His victory, so will you rule in the midst of your enemies.

PART TWO

THE BATTLEGROUND OF THE CHURCH

The other born-again congregations in our cities are not our enemies! We must learn to war against the illusions and strife, the fears and jealousies that are sent from hell to divide us. If Jesus is eternally praying for our oneness (see John 17:20–23), then we must recognize that Satan is continually fighting against it. The devil knows that when we become one with Christ and, through Him, one with each other, it is only a matter of time before this Jesus-built church will destroy the empire of hell!

CHAPTER 8

THE LORD WHOSE SWORD IS DRAWN

Of all the names that the heavenly Father could have given His Son, it is most significant that He chose the name "Jesus," for Jesus is the Greek form of "Joshua." Joshua, you recall, was the Hebrew general who led God's people into war. To be prepared for greater victories, we need a greater revelation of Jesus Christ; we need to see Him as He will be revealed in the last moments of this age: a Holy Warrior, dressed for battle.

WILL YOU RECOGNIZE JESUS WHEN HE COMES?

Now it came about when Joshua was by Jericho, that he lifted up his eyes and looked, and behold, a man was standing opposite him with his sword drawn in his hand,

and Joshua went to him and said to him, "Are you for us or for our adversaries?"   —Joshua 5:13

There is something about the time just prior to a move of God that causes many to wonder if the Lord is for them or against them. He seems confrontational, too intense, too "different" from the One we have learned to trust. Yet, during these last few years, this is exactly the situation in the Lord's relationship with the church. The Lord has stood before us with His sword drawn. He is calling us to follow Him in war.

Perhaps you have been through a time where the tip of Christ's sword seemed aimed straight at your heart. Let me reassure you, God is for you. In fact, it is His expressed purpose to release this same sword of the Spirit, which is the Word of God (see Ephesians 6:17), through your words and prayers. But before the Lord's sword will come through your mouth, it must first pass through your heart.

Do not withdraw or be terrified at this new unveiling of the Son of God, for He is, in fact, fitting you for battle. By the time you are fully trained, you will be a fearless warrior in His army. Yet we must be realistic about our current state: most of us have been pampered and undisciplined. We have not understood the day of warfare that looms before us. Nor are we prepared for the final raging of Satan as his time shortens (see Revelation 12:12).

Isaiah tells us that "the Lord will go forth like a warrior, He will arouse His zeal like a man of war. He will utter a shout, yes, He will raise a war cry. He will prevail against His enemies" (Isaiah 42:13). We have known the Lord as our Savior and our Shepherd. These revelations of our beloved Master are no less true because a new aspect of His nature is revealed. It is simply that this new dimension is so startlingly different from how we have known Him. Be of good cheer, this frightening

Warrior King, with His sword drawn, with the shout of war upon His lips, is the same blessed Savior who died on the cross for our sins.

Yet, in truth, we cannot soften the shock of this great unveiling of Christ. Our immediate dismay shall be in no way less dramatic than that which was revealed to Joshua on the plains of Jericho. Our concepts will be shaken and fears confronted.

Looking again at Joshua, truly he had already known the Lord in a wonderful, intimate way in the wilderness tabernacle. But here, standing before him, was a new revelation of the Lord. The Son of God Himself had come as Captain of the Host to lead His people into war.

Ultimately, these refugees from Egypt and their wilderness children would defeat many nations stronger and more numerous than themselves (see Deuteronomy 9:1). They would do the impossible through the power of the Lord.

Though initially Joshua was taken aback, both Joshua and the people with him were more prepared for this battle than they realized. Their time in the wilderness had conditioned them for war.

Likewise, the wilderness for you has not been a time of punishment but a season of preparation and of learning obedience. You have watched in fear the decline and spiritual death of church leaders who repeatedly disobeyed the Lord. But you have not stumbled over their disobedience; you have learned from it. Today, you walk in the fear of God and are not blinded by the sin of presumption.

Before Jesus returns, those who have passed the wilderness tests will receive another revelation: Christ will be revealed to them as Captain of the Host. They will be ready to follow the Lamb wherever He goes.

> And Joshua fell on his face to the earth, and bowed down, and said to him, "What has my lord to say to his servant?" The captain of the Lord's host said to Joshua, "Remove your sandals from your feet, for the place where you are standing is holy." And Joshua did so.
>
> —Joshua 5:14–15

This new unveiling of the Lord is holy. Overnight the Lord brought down atheistic communism in the former Soviet Union. Since then, hundreds of millions of people from many nations have found salvation in the Son of God. God is touching many nations. Let us not gainsay nor criticize what we may not fully understand. We are beginning to perceive the Lord as He truly is and as He will be released in the last days. He is the Lord of Hosts.

The promise of the Lord, which we read earlier, is that He "will go forth like a warrior . . . He will raise a war cry. He will prevail against His enemies" (Isaiah 42:13). Within the ranks of the advancing church, Jesus is raising a war cry. Can you hear His shout in the intercession? There is new authority being raised up, a new generation whose voice thunders with the cry of prophetic prayer. Through the church, Christ Himself is prevailing against His enemies. Indeed, the gates of hell shall not stand against the church Jesus is building (see Matthew 16:18). The hour has come for us to grow in all aspects into Him, who is our head, even Christ, the Warrior King! (see Ephesians 4:15)

CHAPTER 9

BEWARE OF THE STRONGHOLD OF COLD LOVE

Is your love growing and becoming softer, brighter, more daring and more visible? Or is it becoming more discriminating, more calculating, less vulnerable and less available? This is a very important issue, for your Christianity is only as real as your love. A measurable decrease in your ability to love is evidence that a stronghold of cold love is developing within you.

GUARD AGAINST UNFORGIVENESS!

"Because lawlessness is increased, most people's love will grow cold" (Matthew 24:12). A major area of spiritual warfare that has come against the church is the sphere of church relationships. Satan knows that a church divided against itself cannot stand. We may enjoy temporary blessings and seasonal breakthroughs, but to win a citywide war, Jesus is raising up a united, citywide church. An earmark of this corporate, overcoming church will be its commitment to love. Yet, because of the increasing iniquity in the end of this age, true Christian love will be severely assaulted.

There is no spiritual unity, and hence no lasting victory, without love. Love is a passion for oneness. Bitterness, on the other hand, is characterized by a noticeable lack of love. This cold love is a demonic stronghold. In our generation cold love is becoming increasingly more common. It shuts down the power of prayer and disables the flow of healing and outreach. In fact, where there is persistent and hardened unforgiveness in a person or church, the demonic world (known in Matthew 18:34 as "torturers") has unhindered access.

The Scriptures warn that even a little root of bitterness springing up in a person's life can defile many (see Hebrews 12:15). Bitterness is unfulfilled revenge. Another's thoughtlessness or cruelty may have wounded us deeply. It is inevitable that, in a world of increasing harshness and cruelty, we will at some point be hurt. But if we fail to react with love and forgiveness, if we retain in our spirit the debt the offender owes, that offense will rob our hearts of their capacity to love. Imperceptibly, we will become a member of the majority of end-time Christians whose love is growing cold.

Bitterness is the most visible symptom of the stronghold of cold love. To deal with cold love, we must repent and forgive the one who hurt us. Painful experiences are allowed by God to teach us how to love our enemies. If we still have unforgiveness toward someone, we have failed this test. Fortunately, it was just a test, not a final exam. We actually need to thank God for the opportunity to grow in divine love. Thank Him that your whole life is not being swallowed up in bitterness and resentment. Millions of souls are swept off into eternal judgment every day without any hope of escaping from embitterment, but you have been given God's answer for your pain. God gives you a way out: love!

As we embrace God's love and begin to walk in Christlike forgiveness, we are actually pulling down the stronghold of cold love in our lives. Because of this experience, we will soon possess more of the love of Christ than we had previously.

LOVE WITHOUT COMMITMENT IS NOT LOVE

And at that time many will fall away and will betray one another and hate one another. Many false prophets will arise and will mislead many. Because lawlessness is increased, most people's love will grow cold.
—Matthew 24:10–12

Allow me to be perfectly clear: there is no such thing as love without commitment. *The measure of one's love is found in the depth of his or her commitment to others.* How often we have heard people say, "I loved once, but I was hurt." Or, "I was committed to Christian service, but they used me." When someone withdraws his commitment to a relationship, he is withdrawing his love. It is not one's commitment that grows cold; it is their love. It may not seem like they have become cold—they may still attend church, sing and look "Christian"—but inside they have become hard and separated from others. They have withdrawn from love. Because their commitment is shallow, they will be easily offended.

Jesus said, "It is inevitable that stumbling blocks come" (Matthew 18:7). In your walk there will be times when even good people have bad days. As long as you live on earth, there will never be a time when "stumbling blocks" cease to be found upon your path. People do not stumble over boulders but over stones—little things. To stumble is to stop walking and fall. Have you stumbled over someone's weakness or sin lately? Have you gotten back up and continued loving as you did before, or has that fall caused you to withdraw somewhat from walking after love? To preserve the quality of love in your heart, you must forgive those who have caused you to stumble.

Every time you refuse to forgive or fail to overlook a weakness in another, your heart not only hardens toward them, it hardens toward God. You cannot form a negative opinion of someone (even though you think they may deserve it!) and allow that opinion to crystalize into an attitude; for every time you do, an aspect of your heart will cool toward God. You may still think you are open to God, but the Scriptures are clear: "The one who does not love his brother whom he has seen, cannot love God whom he has not seen" (1 John 4:20). You may not like what someone has done, but you do not have an option to stop loving them. Love is your only choice.

What do I mean by love? First, I do not merely mean "tough love." I mean gentle, affectionate, sensitive, open, persistent love. God will be tough when He needs to be, and we will be firm when He tells us to be, but beneath our firmness must be an underground river of love waiting to spring into action. By *love*, I mean a compassion that is empowered by faith and prayer to see God's best come forth in the people I love. When I have love for someone, I have predetermined that I am going to stand with them, regardless of what they are going through. I am committed.

We each need people who love us, who are committed to us in spite of our imperfections. The fullness of Christ will not come without Christians standing with each other in love. We are not talking about salvation, but growing in salvation until we care for each other, even as Christ has committed Himself to us.

Many people will stumble over little faults and human weaknesses. These minor things are quickly pumped up by the enemy into great big problems. Oh, how frail are the excuses people use to justify withdrawing from others. In reality, these problems, often with a church or pastor, are a smokescreen which masks the person's lack of love.

We need to overcome our hang-ups about commitment, for no one will attain the fullness of God's purposes on earth without being committed to imperfect people along the way.

"Well, as soon as I find a church that believes as I do, I will be committed." This is a dangerous excuse, because as soon as you decide you do not want to forgive, or God begins to deal with the quality of your love, you will blame your withdrawing on some minor doctrinal difference. The kingdom of God is not based on mere doctrines, it is founded upon relationships —relationships with God and, because of God, with one another. Doctrines only help define those relationships. We are not anti-doctrine, but we are against *empty* doctrines which seem like virtues but are simply excuses that justify cold love.

THE GREATEST COMMANDMENTS

An expert in the Law once asked Jesus which was the greatest commandment. His reply was wonderful: " 'You shall love the Lord your God with all your heart, and with all your soul, and with all your mind, and with all your strength.' The second is this, 'You shall love your neighbor as yourself' " (Mark 12:30–31). Jesus said that the second commandment is like the first. When you love God, your love for others will actually be like your love for God. The more you unconditionally love God, the more you will unconditionally love others.

To those whose attitude is, "I am content with just Jesus and me," I say it is wonderful you found Jesus. But you cannot truly have Jesus and simultaneously not do what He says. The outgrowth of love and faith *in* Christ is love and faith *like* Christ's, which means we are committed, even as He is, to His people.

You see, the kingdom of God is most perfectly revealed in our relationships with one another. We are being perfected into a unit (see John 17). To have the kingdom, we must be committed to one another as individuals and as churches. If Christ accepts us while we are still imperfect, we must also accept one another. The people who possess the kingdom of God in its reality are people who overcome the obstacles of each other's faults. They help each other become what God has called them to be: the living body of Jesus Christ.

Remember, the goal of pulling down the stronghold of cold love is to see the oneness of Christ's body revealed. You will be challenged in this, but if you persist, you will discover the height and depth, the length and breadth of Christ's love. You will become a body filled and flooded with God Himself.

CHAPTER 10

THE GIFT
OF DISCERNMENT

*The Holy Spirit will open up the timeless truths of the
Bible; He will also speak to our inner man in dreams, visions
and prophetic words. Yet, much of what God reveals must
pass through the filter of our degree of purity of heart. Thus,
if we will move in true discernment, our view of life must be
purged of human thoughts and reactions. We must perceive
life through the eyes of Christ.*

TO DISCERN, YOU CANNOT JUDGE

We will never possess true discernment until we crucify our
instincts to judge. Realistically, this can take months or even
years of uprooting old thought-systems that have not been
planted in the divine soil of faith and love for people. To
appropriate the discernment which is in the "mind of Christ"

(see 1 Corinthians 2:16), we must first find the heart of Christ. The heart and love of Jesus is summed up in His own words: "I did not come to judge the world, but to save the world" (John 12:47).

Spiritual discernment is the grace to see into the unseen. It is a gift of the Spirit to perceive the realm of the spirit. Its purpose is to understand the nature of that which is veiled. However, the first veil that must be removed is the veil over our own hearts. For the capacity to see into that which is in another's heart comes from Christ revealing that which is in our own hearts. Before He reveals the sin of another, Jesus demands we grasp our own deep need of His mercy. Thus, out of the grace which we have received, we can compassionately minister grace to others. We will know thoroughly that the true gift of discernment is not a faculty of our minds.

Christ's goal is to save, not judge. We are called to navigate the narrow and well-hidden path into the true nature of men's needs. If we would truly help men, we must remember, we are following a Lamb.

This foundation must be laid correctly, for in order to discern, you cannot react. To perceive, you must make yourself blind to what seems apparent. People may react to you, but you cannot react to them. You must always remain forgiving in nature, for the demons you cast out will challenge you, masquerading as the very voice of the person you seek to deliver. You must discern the difference between the oppressing spirit and the person oppressed.

Thus, Jesus prepared His disciples to be proactive in their forgiveness. Using Himself as their example, He taught, "Everyone who speaks a word against the Son of Man, it will be forgiven him" (Luke 12:10). Jesus prepared His heart to forgive men before they ever sinned against Him. He knew His mission was to die for men, not condemn them.

Likewise, we are called to His mission as well. In His prayer to the Father, Jesus said, "As You sent Me into the world, I also have sent them" (John 17:18). We are called to die that others may live. Therefore, we must realize that before our perception develops, our love must mature until our normal attitude is one of forgiveness. Should God reveal to us the hearts of men and then call us to release them from captivity, we cannot react to what they say. As our perception becomes more like Christ Himself and the secrets of men's hearts are revealed to us, we cannot even react to what they *think.*

If we do not move in divine forgiveness, we will walk in much deception. We will presume we have discernment when, in truth, we are seeing through the veil of a critical spirit. We must know our weaknesses, for if we are blind to our sins, what we assume we discern in men will merely be the reflection of ourselves. Indeed, if we do not move in love, we will actually become a menace to the body of Christ.

This is exactly what Jesus taught when He said:

Do not judge so that you will not be judged. For in the way you judge, you will be judged; and by your standard of measure, it will be measured to you. Why do you look at the speck that is in your brother's eye, but do not notice the log that is in your own eye? Or how can you say to your brother, "Let me take the speck out of your eye," and behold, the log is in your own eye? You hypocrite, first take the log out of your own eye, and then you will see clearly to take the speck out of your brother's eye.
—Matthew 7:1–5

Repentance is the removal of the "logs" within our vision; it is the true beginning of seeing clearly. There are many who suppose they are receiving the Lord's discernment concerning one thing or another. Perhaps in some things they are; only God knows. But many are simply judging others and calling it discernment. Jesus commanded us to judge not. The same eternal hand that wrote the Law on stones in the old covenant is writing the law of the kingdom on tablets of flesh today. This word to "not judge" is just as immutably final as His Ten Commandments. It is still God speaking.

THE GOAL IS TO SEE CLEARLY

The judgmental carnal mind always sees the image of itself in others. Without realizing it is seeing itself, it assumes it is perceiving others. Jesus refers to the person who judges as a "hypocrite." The Lord is not saying we should totally stop thinking about people. He wants us to be able to help one another. The emphasis in Jesus' command to "not judge" is summarized in His concluding remark: "First take the log out of your own eye, and then you will see clearly to take the speck out of your brother's eye." *The way we help is not by judging but by seeing clearly.* And we do not see clearly until we have been through deep and thorough repentance, until the instinct to judge after the flesh is uprooted.

We have seen that Jesus paralleled speaking to people about their sins with taking specks out of their eyes. The eye is the most tender, most sensitive part of the human body. How do you take a speck out of someone's eye? *Very carefully!* First, you must win their trust. This means consistently demonstrating an attitude that does not judge, one that will not instinctively condemn. To help others, we must see clearly.

If you seek to have a heart that does not condemn, you must truly crucify your instinct to judge. Then you will have laid a true foundation for the gift of discernment, for you will have prepared your heart to receive the dreams, visions and insights from God. You will be unstained by human bias and corruption.

CHAPTER 11

ELIMINATING
FALSE DISCERNMENT

If what you have to say to someone is very important, you will require their undivided attention. With few exceptions, so also the Holy Spirit does not speak to us until we slow down, tune out the static, and give Him our heart in focused attention. To walk in true discernment, we must be quiet before God. We must learn how to listen.

CEASE STRIVING AND KNOW

The Lord desires we learn how to wait and listen for His voice. He draws our focus to His unlimited power. He admonishes us, "Cease striving and know that I am God" (Psalm 46:10). We cannot engage in spiritual warfare without first becoming conscious of, and submitted to, God. It is through Him that we gain insight into the activity of the enemy. All true discernment comes through a heart that has ceased striving, a heart that knows, even in the fiery trial of its personal struggle, that the Lord is God.

There is a "jamming station," made up of our own thoughts and reactions, that inhibits our powers of discernment. Until the motor of the carnal mind is turned off, true discernment will not consistently be ours. We must die to personal judgments, ideas of retaliation and self-motivation. Indeed, Jesus said, "I can do nothing on My own initiative. As I hear, I judge" (John 5:30); He ceased striving. We also must learn to listen to the voice of the Holy Spirit. As we stop our striving, as we hear God, we discern and judge rightly.

ABOUNDING LOVE BRINGS DISCERNMENT WITH IT

Paul wrote, "I pray that your love may abound still more and more in real knowledge and all discernment" (Philippians 1:9). Discernment comes from abounding love. What is abounding love? It is love that leaps out from us toward others. It is motivated by long-term commitment; it is anointed by sacrificial charity.

There is a false discernment that is based on mistrust, suspicion and fear. You can recognize false discernment by the coldness around it. False discernment may be packaged in a type of love, but it does not originate in love; it comes out of criticism. True discernment is rooted deeply in love.

Picture, if you will, a long-haired young man. His clothes are unkempt and he has tattoos on his arms. It is night and he is walking toward you on a lonely street. It is easy to judge such a person after the obvious and superficial. Now look at this young man in the same setting, but as his mother. You can still see his outer appearance, but when you look at him, you have insight into his life and hope for his future. You see a little boy growing up without a father, a child rejected often by his friends. You have a commitment toward this man that runs deep, has been sustained by love, and that you have carried since you suffered in giving him birth.

False discernment sees the outside of the person or situation and pretends it knows the inside. Godly discernment comes from having godly motives; godly motives are those rooted in God's committed love. In like manner, our capacity to discern the needs of the church will never rise higher than that which is superficial if we do not know Christ's heart for His people.

Jesus said, "Do not judge according to appearance, but judge with righteous judgment" (John 7:24). Righteous judgment is the direct result of love. If you cannot pray in love for a person or the church, do not presume you have true discernment. Love precedes peace, and peace precedes perception. Without love and peace in your heart, your judgment will be overly harsh. Regardless of the smile upon your face, your heart will have too much anger. False discernment is always slow to hear, quick to speak, and quick to anger.

PEACE MUST RULE OUR HEARTS

There is a tension underlying false discernment, an anxiety that pressures the mind to make a judgment. True discernment emerges out of a tranquil and pure heart, one that is almost surprised by the wisdom and grace in the voice of Christ. Remember, our thoughts will always be colored by the attitudes of our hearts. Jesus said, "The mouth speaks out of that which fills the heart" (Matthew 12:34). He also said, "Out of the heart of men, proceed the evil thoughts" (Mark 7:21). Again He said, "the pure in heart . . . shall see God" (Matthew 5:8). From the heart the mouth speaks, the eyes see, and the mind thinks. In fact, Proverbs 4:23 (NKJV) tells us to diligently guard our hearts for "out of [the heart] spring the issues of life."

Life, as we perceive it, is based upon the condition of our heart. This is very important because the gifts of the Spirit must pass through our hearts before they are presented to the world around us. In other words, if our hearts are not right, the gifts will not be right either.

When the heart has unrest it cannot hear from God. Therefore, we must learn to mistrust our judgment when our heart is bitter, angry, ambitious or harboring strife for any reason. The Scriptures tell us to "let the peace of Christ rule [act as arbiter] in [our] hearts" (Colossians 3:15). To hear clearly from God, we must first have peace.

Solomon wrote, "One hand full of rest is better than two fists full of labor and striving after wind" (Ecclesiastes 4:6). There is too much labor and toil in our minds, too much striving after the wind. If we want discernment we must become aggressively calm. This is not a passive state of mind but an expectant, focused waiting upon God. Discernment comes from our sensitivity to Christ in the realm of the Spirit. It comes as we allow love to be our motivation and secure the peace of Christ in our hearts. Through a life so prepared by God, the gift of discernment is revealed.

CHAPTER 12

REPAIRERS OF THE BREACH

And those from among you will rebuild the ancient
ruins; You will raise up the age-old foundations;
And you will be called the repairer of the breach,
The restorer of the paths in which to dwell.
—Isaiah 58:12

THE GATHERING TOGETHER OF THE SAINTS

True Christians from all backgrounds share an expectation commonly known as the rapture of the church (see 1 Thessalonians 4:16). Although debate surrounds the timing of this event, Scripture assures us that it will occur when Jesus Himself returns.

However, before we are "caught up" to meet the Lord, there will be an unusual season of grace in which the living church of

Jesus Christ, like a bride, makes "herself ready" (see Revelation 19:7). In this unparalleled season of preparation, while we will not become perfect, we shall realize a new level of holiness of the quality in which Jesus Himself walked (see 1 Thessalonians 3:11–13; Ephesians 5:26–27; Philippians 1:9–10).

The result of this new spiritual fullness will be a new level of unity. Faultfinding and gossip will disappear. In their place will be intercession and love. Wholeness will return to the citywide church. This also means that the ambition and division we see today between congregations will be identified as sin, which will be repented of before Jesus returns.

The truth of this message must be made clear, for most Christians consider oneness within the body inconceivable before Jesus returns. They have not discerned nor warred against the enemy's lies, which have conditioned believers to accept strife and sectarianism in the church. It is my passionate conviction that the church which will ultimately be raptured will be free of strife and carnal divisions—it will be a bride "having no spot or wrinkle," made ready for her bridegroom (Ephesians 5:27; see Revelation 19:7).

According to Scripture, during the rapture, "in a twinkling of an eye" our bodies will be changed (1 Corinthians 15:52). But our character, that is, the essence of who we have become, will remain intact. There will be no regrets or wondering how "those from that church" made it, for the living bride will be a church built together in love, meeting in separate buildings but serving the one and only Lord. These true disciples of the Lord Jesus will be known for their intense and holy love for one another —not merely in their individual local assemblies but within the context of a citywide church.

It is highly significant that the scriptural term for the rapture is called the "gathering together" (2 Thessalonians 2:1; Matthew 24:31). What ultimately will be consummated in our gathering together physically to the Lord will be precipitated by a spiritual gathering together of His body on earth. Concerning the era known as the "end of the age," Jesus taught that the "good fish" shall be "gathered . . . into containers" (Matthew 13:48). And in the context of spiritual warfare, Jesus warned, "He who does not gather with Me scatters" (Matthew 12:30).

This scattering, dividing process among the Lord's sheep has gone on long enough. Jesus has set His heart to bring healing and unity to His body. In this regard, through the prophet Jeremiah, the Lord spoke a somber warning. He said, "Woe to the shepherds who are destroying and scattering the sheep of My pasture!" (Jeremiah 23:1) The Son of God is not pleased with the carnal divisions in His body! Indeed, the Lord promises to chasten those pastors who continue to build their kingdoms without laboring together to build His. To them He says, "I am about to attend to you for the evil of your deeds" (v. 2).

In the tenth chapter of John, the Lord makes His goal clear: there shall be "one flock with one shepherd" (v. 16). He reveals that it is the wolf nature which "snatches [the sheep] and scatters them"; and it is the hireling nature which allows the scattering to occur. But His promise to His sheep says this:

Then I Myself will gather the remnant of My flock and they will be fruitful and multiply. I will also raise up shepherds over them and they will tend them; and they will not be afraid any longer . . . nor will any be missing.
—Jeremiah 23:3–4

The pastors of the last Christian church will be under-shepherds to the Lord Jesus; they will be anointed to gather together His remnant and under that anointing shall be "fruitful and multiply."

Indeed, right now, in the context of humbling ourselves and submitting our hearts to His will, we are participating in being "gathered together." This process will progressively increase until the barriers between brethren are melted by the overcoming nature of Christ's love. Before Jesus returns, we will truly be "one flock with one shepherd." We will be a holy and blameless sheepfold, meeting in different buildings but baptized into one body.

DO NOT CRITICIZE THE BREACH, REPAIR IT!

"Thus says the Lord God, 'Woe to the foolish prophets who are following their own spirit and have seen nothing. O Israel, your prophets have been like foxes among ruins. You have not gone up into the breaches, nor did you build the wall around the house of Israel to stand in the battle on the day of the Lord.' "   —Ezekiel 13:3–5

God needs people who, when they see a gap in the citywide church wall, will go up into the breaches and rebuild the wall so that the church will stand in the day of battle. In every city, town and village, each of us needs the other churches if we are going to stand in the day of battle.

You may be thinking, "You don't understand, I have revelation of the end-time move of God. These churches barely believe in Jesus." The Word tells us that "without any dispute the lesser is blessed by the greater" (Hebrews 7:7). If you are truly "greater," without a hint of pride you will seek ways to be a blessing to other churches. Your Christlike love will cast out fears. You will sincerely have a burden to see the entire body of Christ brought forth, not just your local assembly; you will respect the diversity of ways through which Christ reveals

Himself in the church. In truth, Jesus said that the greatest among us would become the "servant of all" (Mark 9:35).

If a church in your city holds to and confesses Jesus as their Lord and Savior, then that church is needed to complete God's work in the city. As you join one another for daily or weekly prayer, you will be blessed and surprised by God's preparation of others. Do not come with an attitude to teach or lead, but to love and serve. In this, God is not looking for leaders but followers of the Lord Jesus Christ.

If we do not adjust to His will, we will be unable to stand against the enemy. Indeed, the day in which we live is not a day of peace, it is a time of war. God is gathering us together not only to Him and each other but also against the spiritual forces of wickedness in every region. Therefore, the breaches between us must be filled, the walls built, and we must learn to stand together in the day of the Lord.

YOU BE THE PEOPLE

You do not have to go to Bible college to find fault with the church. In fact, if you remember, you could find fault with the church even before you were a Christian. You do not need skill to find fault. But if you want to be like Christ, you have to be willing to lay your life down for people's sins. You have to be an intercessor who "stands in the gap." *The "gap" is the distance between the way things are and the way things should be.* You stand in that space, cast down the accuser of the brethren, and intercede! Have you seen something that is wrong? It is only because Jesus wants you to stand in the gap and pray to see it changed.

Some of us have cried for years, "Where are those who will lead us into Christ's fullness?" We have assumed that God had others in mind. What the Lord is saying, however, is, *You be the men and women that others are looking for.* You be the peacemakers, the sons and daughters of God that bring healing, honor and order to His church.

The responsibility is upon each of us. There is a tremendous job ahead, but the Lord Himself has promised, "Those from among you will rebuild the ancient ruins; you will raise up the age-old foundations; and you will be called the repairer of the breach, the restorer of the paths in which to dwell" (Isaiah 58:12).

Let us lay our lives down in committed faith, believing that in our lifetimes, on this earth and in our communities, the corporate church of Jesus Christ will be restored, united and made ready as a bride for her Beloved!

CHAPTER 13

GOD'S ARMY OF WORSHIPERS

When the Scriptures refer to the "heavenly host," we usually think of "choirs of angels." The word "host" in the Bible meant "army" (Joshua 5:13–14). It is an important truth: the hosts of heaven are worshiping armies. Indeed, no one can do warfare who is not first a worshiper of God.

THE CENTRAL ISSUE IN TRIBULATION: WORSHIP

One does not have to penetrate deeply into the Revelation of John to discover that both God and the devil are seeking worshipers (see Revelation 7:11; 13:4; 14:7,11). Time and time again the line is drawn between those who "worship the beast and his image" and those who worship God.

In the last great battle before Jesus returns, the outcome of every man's life shall be weighed upon a scale of worship: in the midst of warfare and battles to whom will we bow, God or Satan?

Yet, while this warfare shall culminate in the establishment of the Lord's kingdom on earth (see Revelation 11:15), we must realize the essence of this battle is the central issue in our warfare today. Will we faithfully worship God during satanic assault and temptation? True worship must emerge now in the context of our daily lives, for no man will worship through the great battles of tomorrow who complains in the mere skirmishes of today.

You will remember that the Lord's call to the Israelites was a call to worship and serve Him in the wilderness (see Exodus 7:16). Indeed, when Moses first spoke of God's loving concern, we read that the Hebrews "bowed low and worshiped" (Exodus 4:31). But when trials and pressures came, they fell quickly into murmuring, complaining and blatant rebellion. Their worship was superficial, self-serving and conditional—a form without a heart of worship.

This same condition of shallow worship prevails in much of Christianity today. If a message is given that speaks of the Lord's great care for His people, with eagerness do we bow low and worship. But as soon as the pressures of daily living arise or temptations come, how quickly we rebel against God and resist His dealings! The enemy has easy access to the soul that is not protected by true worship of the Almighty! Indeed, the Lord's purpose with Israel in the wilderness was to perfect true worship, which is based upon the reality of God, not circumstances. The Lord knows that the heart that will worship Him in the wilderness of affliction will continue to worship in the promised land of plenty.

Without true worship of God, there can be no victory in warfare. For what we bleed when we are wounded by satanic assault or difficult circumstances is the true measure of our worship. You see, what comes out of our hearts during times of pressure is in us, but hidden during times of ease. If you are a true worshiper, your spirit will exude worship to God no matter what battle you are fighting. In warfare, worship creates a wall of fire around the soul.

PROTECTING YOUR HEART THROUGH WORSHIP

Most of us understand the basic dynamics of the human soul. We have been taught, and rightly so, that the soul is the combination of our mind, will and emotions. Generally speaking, when the enemy comes against the church, he targets any of these three areas. We must see that the protection of these areas is of vital importance in our war against Satan.

To further illuminate the nature of this battle, let us add that, in addition to the mind, the will and the emotions, the soul is made of events and how we responded to those events. Who we are today is the sum of what we have encountered in life and our subsequent reactions. Abuses and afflictions hammer us one way, encouragement and praise inflate us another. Our reaction to each event, whether that event was positive or negative, is poured into the creative marrow of our individuality, where it is blended into the nature of our character.

What we call *memory* is actually our spirit gazing at the substance of our soul. With few exceptions, those events that we remember the most have also shaped us the most. Indeed, the reason our natural minds cannot forget certain incidents is because those events have literally become part of our nature.

Our soul, its strengths and weaknesses, has been shaped by how well or poorly we handled our past experiences. When Scripture commands us to not look back and to "forget... what lies behind" (Philippians 3:13; see Luke 9:62), it is saying we must undo the consequences that have come from our unchristlike reactions. With God, this is not impossible, *for although the events of our lives are irreversible, our reactions to those events can still be changed.* As our wrong reactions to the past change, we change. In other words, although we cannot alter the past, we can put our past upon the "altar" as an act of worship. A worshiping heart truly allows God to restore the soul.

All of us receive a portion of both good and evil in this world. But for life to be good, God, who is the essence of life, must reach into our experiences and redeem us from our negative reactions. The channel through which the Lord extends Himself, even into our past, is our love and worship of Him.

"And we know that God causes all things to work together for good to those who love God" (Romans 8:28). The key for the fulfillment of this verse is that we become lovers of God in our spirits. Bad things become good for "those who love God." When we are given to loving Him, all that we have passed through in life is washed and redeemed in that love. Bad becomes good by the power of God.

Therefore, it is essential to both the salvation of our souls and our protection in warfare that we be worshipers. The ship which safely carries us through the storms of adversity is worship.

Psalm 84 expresses in praise to God the wonderful effect worship has upon the soul. "How blessed is the man whose strength is in You, in whose heart are the highways to Zion! Passing through the valley of Baca [weeping] they make it a spring; the early rain also covers it with blessings" (v. 5–6).

If you are "ever praising" God (Psalm 84:4), your worship of God will transform the negative assault of the enemy into "a spring" of sweet refreshing waters. No matter what befalls a worshiper, their "valley of weeping" always becomes a spring covered "with blessings." You cannot successfully engage in warfare, nor pass safely through the wilderness of this life, without first becoming a worshiper of God.

WORSHIP: THE PURPOSE OF CREATION

We were created for God's pleasure. We were not created to live for ourselves but for Him. And while the Lord desires that we enjoy His gifts and His people, He would have us know we were created first for His pleasure. In these closing moments of this age, the Lord will have a people whose purpose for living is to please God with their lives. In them, God finds His own reward for creating man. They are His worshipers. They are on earth only to please God, and when He is pleased, they also are pleased.

The Lord takes them farther and through more pain and conflicts than other men. Outwardly, they often seem "smitten of God, and afflicted" (Isaiah 53:4). Yet to God, they are His beloved. When they are crushed, like the petals of a flower, they exude a worship, the fragrance of which is so beautiful and rare that angels weep in quiet awe at their surrender. They are the Lord's purpose for creation.

One would think that God would protect them, guarding them in such a way that they would not be marred. Instead, they are marred more than others. Indeed, the Lord seems pleased to crush them, putting them to grief. For in the midst of their physical and emotional pain, their loyalty to Christ grows pure and perfect. And in the face of persecutions, their love and worship toward God become all-consuming.

Would that all Christ's servants were so perfectly surrendered. Yet God finds His pleasure in us all. But as the days of the kingdom draw near and the warfare at the end of this age increases, those who have been created solely for the worship of God will come forth in the power and glory of the Son. With the high praises of God in their mouth, they will execute upon His enemies the judgment written (see Psalm 149). They will lead as generals in the Lord's army of worshipers.

CHAPTER 14

CASTING DOWN
THE ACCUSER
OF THE BRETHREN

Jesus calls us beyond the standards of "church as usual"; He calls us to reveal the life and power of the kingdom of God. What is the difference between the church and God's kingdom? Those who seek first for God's kingdom are love-motivated people who are given to prayer. When they see a need, instead of judging, they intercede.

HOW THE KINGDOM COMES

Now the salvation, and the power, and the kingdom of our God and the authority of His Christ have come, for the accuser of our brethren has been thrown down, who accuses them before our God day and night.

—Revelation 12:10

There will be an actual point in time when the "salvation," "power" and "kingdom of God," as well as the "authority of Christ," are manifested in the earth. While we wait patiently for the fulfillment of that glorious event, the spirit of this eternal reality can be possessed any time a people determine to walk free of criticism and faultfinding, and turn their sights toward purity, love and prayer for each other.

There are God-ordained procedures to initiate correction within a church. These corrections should be done by "you who are spiritual . . . in a spirit of gentleness; . . . looking to yourself, so that you too will not be tempted." Your motive should be to "restore such a one" (Galatians 6:1). Accusations against an elder, though, should not even be received "except on the basis of two or three witnesses" (1 Timothy 5:19). The "witnesses" spoken of here are actual eye-witnesses, not merely "intuitive" witnesses people might have apart from hard and visible facts. All too often, these alleged "witnesses" are critical people manipulated by hell to destroy the harmony of a church with rumors and gossip.

When the scriptural approach to rectifying a situation is ignored, it opens the door to fault-finding, fleshly criticisms and judging. The spirit that exploits these sins, according to Revelation 12:10, is called the "accuser of our brethren." Indeed, when the spirit of accusation and criticism is operative, the movement of the Holy Spirit in the church is greatly restricted: salvations are few, power is minimal, and spiritual authority is crippled. Such a church is in serious danger.

Certainly, correction is necessary in the church. Yet, to be truly anointed to bring Christ's corrections to a church, one must be anointed with Christ's redemptive motives. The

Scriptures are plain, Jesus "always lives to make intercession for [the saints]" (Hebrews 7:25; see also Romans 8:34). The Son of God "did not come to judge the world, but to save the world" (John 12:47). Likewise, God does not call us to judge one another, but to pray for one another. If we see a need in the body of Christ, our first reaction should be to intercede and not simply criticize. Our pattern must be to follow Christ in building and restoring, not to echo the accuser of the brethren in merely finding fault.

Many years ago I belonged to a national Christian organization that, in spite of its good points, had several serious problems. At that time I was pastoring a small church and I felt perhaps we should leave this group because of what was wrong. Together, the congregation and I began to seek the Lord with prayer and periods of fasting for forty days. At the end of that time I wrote a list of complaints and, holding them before God, I prayed (somewhat self-righteously), "Lord, look at the errors in these people. Direct us, Lord, what should we do?"

Immediately the Lord replied, "Have you seen these things?"

"Yes, Lord," I answered, "I have seen their sins."

To which He said, "So also have I, but I died for them; you go and do likewise."

From that day on, I found a grace from God to seek to be a source of life and prayer wherever I was serving God. If I truly wanted to be like Jesus, it would never again be enough to simply find fault; I would have to also become an intercessor whose motive was redemption.

You see, we will always be serving in churches where things are wrong. Our response to what we see defines how Christlike we are actually becoming. If we see weakness in the body of Christ, our call is to supply strength. If we see sin, our response is to be an example of virtue. When we discover fear, we must impart courage, and where there is worldliness, we must display holiness. Our call is to enter the place of intercession and stand there until the body of Christ is built up in that area.

IS THE DEVIL AT THE THRONE OF GOD?

Ephesians 2:6 tells us that we have been raised up and are seated "with [Christ] in the heavenly places." Let us understand that, while our bodies and souls are quite fixed here upon earth, through the agency of the Holy Spirit, our spirits have been brought into direct fellowship with Christ in heaven. From this position, we can boldly approach God's throne of grace and we can enter through prayer and worship into the true holy place of God (Hebrews 4:16; 10:19–20; see also Matthew 5:8; Colossians 3:1–4).

There are many Scriptures which support the truth of our positional seating with Christ. It is important for us to understand this, for we are going to examine a doctrine that has been a source of confusion for many saints: is Satan in heaven also? Is he actually standing before the throne of God?

Study the book of Revelation and in the description of God's throne you will find no devil there (see chapter 4). Investigate Hebrews, chapter twelve, and in the discourse concerning the heavenly Jerusalem, again you will see no devil in heaven. To further emphasize this, during a home meeting in Toronto, Canada, while we were in deep worship before the Lord, in varying degrees the Holy Spirit opened to each of us a view into the heavenly Jerusalem. We saw a realm wherein there was neither darkness nor death. Everything was baptized in the living glory of God. There simply was no need of the sun nor of any other light, for everything was alive and within everything was the outraying light of God. We beheld many things, but my point is that there was no darkness nor any devil in heaven.

Where then is Satan? Jude tells us that the devil and his demons are imprisoned, spiritually chained with "eternal bonds" to "darkness [reserved] for the judgment" (Jude 1:6). Satan is imprisoned under darkness. The thought that the heavenly Father, "in [whom] there is no darkness at all" (1 John 1:5), would countenance the devil intruding upon the eternal worship, accusing the very church for whom His Son had died, is unimaginable.

How then do we explain the Scriptures which allude to a devil in heaven? While we freely admit we do not know all the ways in which Satan accuses man before God, we do offer one solution.

First, there are three realms known as heaven in the Bible. The most commonly identified as such is the eternal abode of God, angels and the redeemed. Next, the word *heaven* is used to describe the sky. "The heavens declare the glory of God" (Psalm 19:1 KJV). But when the Bible says that Satan is in heaven or the "heavenly places" (Ephesians 6:12; Revelation 12:7–8; Luke 10:18), we believe it is with reference to the spirit realm, which because of sin and the fall of man also has been invaded by darkness. This heaven is the spiritual territory from which Satan seeks to control the world. It would be foolish to assume we know more than we do about this dimension, but we know this: it is from here that Satan releases his war against the church.

If it is true that the devil is not in the highest heaven, how then does he accuse the saints before the throne of God? We began this discourse by explaining that Christ has positioned our spirits in Him before God's throne. While our spirits connect us to God, our bodies and souls are here on earth.

Although the devil does not have immediate access to God, he does have access to our thoughts and words. When we harbor sympathetic attitudes toward faultfinding, when we justify gossip and negative criticism, we are actually giving Satan the use of our mouths to accuse the saints before God!

We have wrongly assumed that our whispers spoken in darkness remained hidden even from God. We must realize that "all things are open and laid bare to the eyes of Him with whom we have to do" (Hebrews 4:13). Is it not written, "whatever you have said in the dark will be heard in the light" (Luke 12:3)? God, who is Light, indeed hears the voice of the accuser, even in the guarded confidences spoken to a spouse or friend.

GUARD YOUR TONGUE!

Much of what the Father supplies to the body of Christ is furnished through our confession. This is not simply our positive, premeditated confession expressed in prayer; it consists of everything that comes out of our mouths. Did not Christ Himself say men shall be judged for "every idle (or careless) word" that they speak (Matthew 12:36 KJV)?

Our words are the overflow of our hearts. Indeed, God has so structured life that our very words, whether they are spoken in faith or unbelief, play a determinant role in shaping our future. James tells us that the tongue "sets on fire the course of our life, and is set on fire by hell" (James 3:6). If hell can use the tongue for evil, God certainly can use it for good. Scripture tells us, "The one who desires life, to love and see good days, must keep his tongue from evil and his lips from speaking deceit" (1 Peter 3:10).

If we desire life and the blessing of love and good days, we must keep our tongues from speaking evil. We must use our words to support, love and protect each other. If we do, we will experience much growth and greater protection. However, if we are finding fault, criticizing and talebearing, the voice of the accuser is manifested, and we are judged for our idle and evil words. God looks at what we have said and gives us reality accordingly.

Consequently, we must come to understand that each of our thoughts, and even our most intimate conversations with others, are actually prayers we are offering to the Father who sees all things continually and in secret. These unaddressed prayers are just as much a part of our confession as our "Dear Lord" prayers, and they are just as influential. Our words about one another, as well as our words to one another, should carry with them the same sense of reverence as when we speak with God. For He is, indeed, listening.

OTHER TONGUES OR FLAMING TONGUES?

It is significant that when Isaiah saw the Lord (Isaiah 6), not only was there no devil in heaven, but the guilt he felt was due to his words. He said, "Woe is me, for I am ruined! Because I am a man of unclean lips, and I live among a people of unclean lips" (v. 5). The fact is, our criticisms of one another are the voice of Satan accusing the saints before God.

Isaiah's lips were cleansed as they were touched by a burning coal taken from the altar of God. The closer we truly draw to God, the more guilt we shall feel for our unclean words. When the Holy Spirit was manifested upon Jesus, He came symbolically in the form of a dove. But when the Spirit was revealed at Pentecost, He appeared as flaming tongues of fire. Certain segments of Christianity have made speaking in "other tongues" a sign of the infilling of the Holy Spirit. For us, the issue shall not be speaking in foreign tongues, but flaming tongues—tongues which have been purified by the fire of God from the altar, tongues that are cleansed of faultfinding and criticisms.

CASTING DOWN THE ACCUSER

As followers of Jesus Christ we are called to overcome the accuser of the brethren. How do we accomplish this holy task? In Revelation 12:11, we see how the victorious church overcomes the accuser of the brethren. Therefore, let us study this text and let it unlock our victory.

> And they overcame him because of the blood of the Lamb and because of the word of their testimony, and they did not love their life even when faced with death.
> —Revelation 12:11

❏   "The blood of the Lamb." The Lord Jesus shed His blood to establish a new covenant between God and man. That covenant required Christ to offer Himself as a blameless lamb to God for mankind's sins, wherein God would put upon Him the sins of us all.

Our role in this covenant is to accept and believe in what God has done. We are to abandon self-righteousness and put our trust in Christ's righteousness. As a result, we attain an imparted righteousness that is unencumbered by religious pride.

Indeed, the blood covenant ransoms us from the accusations of Satan, while it also convicts us of our tendency to accuse those who sinned against us. Thus, Christ's shed blood delivers us from the realm of accusations and secures us in the life of God's kingdom, for it requires we walk without pride and that we extend mercy to those who have sinned against us (see Matthew 6:12; 18:23–35; Romans 8:31–34).

❑ "The word of their testimony." This includes testifying to others about the works of God, but it is also much more. "The testimony of Jesus," Scripture says, "is the spirit of prophecy" (Revelation 19:10). *In other words, to truly overcome the voice of accusation we must live and think prophetically.*

We view each fellow disciple in Christ's church not according to their fleshly weaknesses but according to the redemptive vision granted us by God's transforming grace. Our testimony is a faith-declaration of God's promise in Scripture: *we are new creatures, we have received the Holy Spirit and the God of heaven is establishing His kingdom in our midst* (see Matthew 24:14; Daniel 2:44).

We overcome the accuser by maintaining faith for each other, even when our brother or sister stumbles or falls. The word of our testimony is that God is good. He is faithful and He will fulfill what He has promised concerning us.

❑ "They loved not our own lives, even unto death." *We cannot love our soul life more than our spirit life.* Without doubt, our vision will be challenged. The devil will raise up people who will come against us; even friends may turn against us. Yet, we cannot react in the flesh.

We must maintain our love and faith, even when we face betrayal or injustice. Again, we cannot love our soul life more than our spirit life. Thus, we cannot overcome Satan and simultaneously harbor self-pity and sympathy for that which needs to be crucified within us. Our victory is consummated by our willingness to go even to death rather than betray our convictions of truth and love.

Paul said, "I do not consider my life of any account as dear to myself, in order that I may finish my course" (Acts 20:24). Those who walk in true spiritual maturity are unsympathetic toward their own wounds. They may hurt, but not withdraw. Yet, because they embrace Christ's cross, they also walk in His kingdom in the resurrection power (see Philippians 3:10–11).

The accuser must be cast down first in our minds. We cannot tolerate faultfinding and accusations. We must possess the very heart of God toward our brethren. The kingdom of God and the authority of His Christ will be seen in a people who are terminally committed to love-motivated prayer. For when they see a need, instead of becoming critical, they cast down the accuser of the brethren, and they pray!

PART THREE

THE BATTLEGROUND OF THE HEAVENLY PLACES

The last frontier of battle is the heavenly places, the dimension known today as the spirit realm. It is here that angels and demons wage their war for our cities. But let the reader take note: this dimension is currently enemy territory! Only according to the measure that our heart is like Christ's do we have authority in the heavenlies; only a citywide, Christ-centered church can displace the powers of darkness from the spirit realm.

Note: It would be helpful to read the glossary at the end of the book for clarity and definition concerning these next chapters.

CHAPTER 15

THE WAR
OVER REALITY

Created in the image of God, man was given limited, yet distinct, inherent powers. He was granted the power to imagine, as well as the faculty to define and then establish reality. And, operating within the boundaries preset by God, man does this, for better or worse, according to the free selection of his will. As we understand this, we see that the essence of spiritual warfare is in who shall define reality: the Word of God or the illusions of this present age.

WHAT WE AGREE UPON

What is reality? How does life appear—to you? The dictionary defines reality as "that which is real; an actual thing, situation, or event." Such is reality in terms of objective analysis. But reality is not just objective: there is also a subjective or personal side to reality which is rooted in our feelings, attitudes, and beliefs. From this perspective, life is "done for [us] as [we] have believed" (Matthew 8:13).

In this personal side of reality, what seems real to one is very often unreal to another. Consider the Eskimo's view of reality: traveling by dog sled and dwelling in an igloo, living in the land of the northern lights and the midnight sun. Compare that to a businessman living in New York City: traveling in subways and automobiles, living in a concrete world of skyscrapers and parking lots, with the stress of rush hours and a high-pressure job in a brokerage firm. Reality in both locations, though strikingly different, is uniquely functional and subjectively real to each individual.

Let us, therefore, learn from these examples an important principle: *whatever a society agrees upon and establishes through consent, compromise and constant use will ultimately define reality to them.* Understanding this precept is very important because, as we come into agreement with the principles and standards of the kingdom of God, our whole definition of society is going to change.

An example of this in Scripture is seen in the book of Genesis. "And the Lord said, Behold, they are one people, and they have all one language; and this is only the beginning of what they will do; and now nothing they have imagined they can do will be impossible to them" (Genesis 11:6 AMP). This is what the Lord Himself said concerning the ungodly Babylonians. He said that *whatever mankind imagined, it had the potential to accomplish.*

If you doubt the validity of that statement, you would have stood among the scoffers when dreamers envisioned themselves standing on the moon. You would have scorned the concept that voices and images could be transmitted around the world through invisible frequencies. Indeed, you would have ridiculed the idea that weapons would become powerful enough to destroy all life on earth. Yet, today these things are part of our world because of man's power to establish reality. *If a man's mind can imagine it and he can get others to believe in it, their spirits can accomplish it.* And with few exceptions, nothing will be impossible, even for as small a group as two or three, once they believe a thing can happen.

This is exactly what the warfare is centered upon in the church today: the devil wants us to accept Christianity as it is, as though division, sin, and spiritual impotency were the ultimate reality God has provided for believers on earth. Satan wants us to *agree with and thereby reinforce* this deceptive view of the church. There are many promises that are yet to be fulfilled concerning the people of God. These are holy and noble purposes which shall unfold in the last days. Therefore, our agreement must be with *God's plan* for a holy, undivided, powerful church, for He is calling us to establish *His* kingdom, not the status quo!

While we must work with the church as it is, we must ever realize that what we see in Christianity is *not* what the church will be like before Jesus returns. In fact, our call is to cooperate with God in the bringing forth of revival and the raising up of the body of Christ. Our quest is to serve the vision of the Lord until He presents "to Himself the church in all her glory, having no spot or wrinkle or any such thing; but that she should be holy and blameless" (Ephesians 5:27).

Before Jesus returns, the Father has promised His Son a bride without spot or wrinkle. She shall be a powerful witness of Christ Himself in the earth.

WAR IN HEAVEN: THE PRINCIPLE OF DISPLACEMENT

"Then war broke out in heaven, Michael and his angels going forth to battle with the dragon; and the dragon and his angels fought, but they were defeated and there was no room found for them in heaven any longer" (Revelation 12:7–8 AMP). Notice the phrase, "there was no room . . . for them in heaven." The war against principalities involves displacement: Christ filling the spiritual territories once held by Satan.

This war in heaven is difficult for us to comprehend. How do angels and demons, beings who do not die from wounds, wage war? With what do they do battle? And how do they conquer one another? Without exceeding the bounds of our knowledge, we can safely say this: *All spiritual warfare is waged over one essential question: Who will control reality on earth, heaven or hell?*

When it comes to angelic and demonic warfare, the battle rests not in physical weaponry but in the *power of agreement* between mankind and the spirit realm. We read in Ephesians 6 (NKJV) that "principalities" and "powers" occupy the "heavenly places" (v. 12). But we read in Ephesians 1:10 that it is the Father's expressed purpose to sum up all things in Christ, "things in the heavens and things on the earth." Ephesians 3:10 reveals God's glorious plan, that *"through the church"* God has purposed to make known His manifold wisdom to the principalities and powers "in the *heavenly places.* " You see, as the body of Christ on earth agrees with its Head in heaven, the Spirit of Christ Himself displaces the powers of darkness in the heavenly places.

In other words, when the church on earth is aggressive in its agreement with the will and Word of God, then the presence of

God increases in the spiritual realm, proportionally displacing the influence of hell on earth. Shortly thereafter, manifesting in the world of men, we see revivals, healings and miracles. But when the church is passive, indifferent or carnal, the powers of hell increase their rule over the affairs of men: marriages break up, crime increases, and wantonness becomes unbridled. We must see that our prayers, attitudes, and agreement with God are an integral part of establishing the reality of the kingdom of God on earth!

THE DEVIL IS A LIAR

Satan is unmasked in Scripture as "a liar and the father of lies" (John 8:44). His realm of operation is the spirit world that immediately surrounds and blankets the consciousness of mankind. This realm is known as the "heavenly places" in the Bible (Ephesians 6:12). From this spiritual realm Satan works to corrupt and control the mind of man through illusions built from mankind's carnal desires and fears. But the power of the lie is not merely the speaking of falsehoods, nor is it that this world is an illusion. The lie of the enemy appears most powerfully when men believe that this world, *as it is*, is the only world we can live in. The truth is, of course, that God is establishing His kingdom and, ultimately, every other reality will submit to and be ruled by that kingdom! (see Hebrews 12:26–28; Revelation 11:15)

The weapon God has given us to combat the lies of the enemy is the Word of God, which the Scriptures refer to as the "sword of the Spirit" (Ephesians 6:17). Jesus said His words "are spirit and are life" (John 6:63), which is to say that the substance or meaning in Christ's words represents an actual reality: the living Spirit of the kingdom of God.

We should also recognize that the ancient Greeks, in whose language the New Testament was written, had no word for "reality." To them "truth" and "reality" were the same essence. If we seek to experience the true work of the Holy Spirit, we should understand that the Spirit has been sent to establish the reality of God's kingdom in the lives of Jesus' followers. Thus, as we become one with the Spirit of Truth, and as we fully embrace the Word of Truth, we are brought into the reality of God Himself!

This point is essential: in our war over who controls man's world, the singular weapon God has given the church is His Spirit-empowered Word. The living Word of the Spirit is the truth.

Paul taught that spiritual warfare deals specifically with the "pulling down of strongholds." But what are those strongholds? They are lies the devil has sown into our thought-processes which, as we accepted and believed them, became reality to us. We do not *fall* in sin as much as we are *seduced* by it; every sin is cloaked in some measure of deception. But, as these lies are uncovered and destroyed, as our thought-processes are freed from illusions, we will discover the blamelessness, perfection, and truth of Christ in us, the hope of glory (see Colossians 1:27).

STANDING UPON THE WORD OF GOD

To be successful in battle, we must know the Word of God. If you are in need of deliverance, or if you are being used in the ministry of deliverance, the following verses will be helpful in establishing victory. It is not wise to engage in any kind of spiritual warfare without knowing these Scriptures perfectly from memory.

For the weapons of our warfare are not carnal, but mighty through God to the pulling down of strong holds; . . .We are destroying speculations and every lofty thing raised up against the knowledge of God, and we are taking every thought captive to the obedience of Christ.
—2 Corinthians 10:4 KJV, 10:5 NAS

"Do not participate in the unfruitful deeds of darkness, but instead even expose them" (Ephesians 5:11). When you expose and confess your sins, they no longer are in darkness (secrecy). When light is turned on in a dark room, darkness becomes light. So also, when you bring your sins out of darkness and expose them to light, they vanish in God's forgiveness; they become light.

"If we confess our sins, He is faithful and righteous to forgive us our sins and to cleanse us from all unrighteousness" (1 John 1:9). Again, confess your sins. God is faithful and just to forgive and to cleanse you of all unrighteousness.

"But thanks be to God, who always leads us in triumph in Christ, and manifests through us the sweet aroma of the knowledge of Him in every place" (2 Corinthians 2:14). There is victory, right here, right now because Christ is in you.

"For God has not given us a spirit of fear, but of power and of love and of a sound mind" (2 Timothy 1:7 NKJV). Do not fear Satan's threats. Always remember, the devil is "a liar" and "there is no truth in him" (John 8:44).

"Through death He might render powerless him who had the power of death, that is, the devil; and might free those who through fear of death were subject to slavery all their lives" (Hebrews 2:14–15). Satan may try to make you believe he has power over you, but Jesus says that Satan has been rendered "powerless" in our lives. Use the name of Jesus and the Word of God to break the power of Satan's lies.

"And we know that God causes all things to work together for good to those who love God, to those who are called according to His purpose" (Romans 8:28). If God causes everything to work for good as you love Him, then ultimately nothing bad can ever happen to you. God has predestined you to be conformed to the image of His Son.

"Behold, I have given you authority to tread on serpents and scorpions, and over all the power of the enemy, and nothing shall injure you" (Luke 10:19). Jesus has given us authority over all of Satan's power. We have His authority and His promise that nothing shall injure us!

"The Son of God appeared for this purpose, to destroy the works of the devil" (1 John 3:8). You have been set free—not because you feel free, but because you have faith. Each time you speak your faith, you are *establishing* your freedom as a true reality. Your confidence is that while you are praying, the angelic hosts of God, which outnumber the devil by at least two to one, are united with you against evil. With Jesus, you cannot fail! (see also Ephesians 6:18; James 4:7; Isaiah 42:13; 53; 54:11–17; Romans 10:8–9)

CHAPTER **16**

EXPOSING THE SPIRIT OF ANTICHRIST!

There is an order of beings whose iron fist rules the empire of hell; their cloud of evil darkens nearly every facet of life on earth. To topple this wicked kingdom and prevail victoriously in our warfare, we must discern our enemies and set to flight these commanders of darkness.

MORE THAN JUST A MAN

There exists a ruler of darkness, a principality of the deadliest order, that has been tolerated by believers for so long that its influence is considered *normal* for the church. This diabolical entity is the spirit of antichrist. While this spirit manifests itself wherever true Christianity is openly persecuted, it is a demon whose nature is primarily religious. This spirit stands firmly in opposition against the unfolding restoration of the church of Jesus Christ.

As this demon's name is, so is he. He is simply "anti" or against Christ. He manifests empty religion as truth instead of the actual life of Christ Himself. This principality uses the power-demons of jealousy, fear, unforgiveness and ambition—whatever is necessary to keep independent, local churches from becoming the "armed and dangerous," *united* body of Christ.

It is easy to lock our interpretation of the antichrist into a particular personage who will be revealed just prior to Christ's return. Indeed, most Christians are in agreement that such a man will ultimately emerge. This individual "opposes and exalts himself above every so-called god or object of worship, so that he takes his seat in the temple of God, displaying himself as being God" (2 Thessalonians 2:4). But, if this is the antichrist in his human, manifested form, then this also describes the nature or essence of the antichrist spirit in its invisible form.

This spirit of antichrist has been prevalent in the church since the first century. In fact, the apostle John plainly states that there were "many antichrists" in the first century. He wrote, "Children, it is the last hour; and just as you heard that antichrist is coming, even now many antichrists have appeared" (1 John 2:18). When we compare this verse with 2 Thessalonians 2:4, we see that our understanding of the term "antichrist" has been too narrow when limited to one man in the future. John said, *"even now* many antichrists have appeared."

It is important to grasp that John is actually speaking of people who once seemed to be members of the united, citywide Christian community. The apostle tells us that "they went out from us." He said, "If they had been of us, they would have remained with us" (1 John 2:19).

What motivated these misled souls? Later in John's epistle, the apostle reveals it was the antichrist spirit. He wrote in chapter four, "Every spirit that does not confess Jesus is not from God; this is the spirit of the antichrist, of which you have heard that it is coming, and now it is already in the world" (1 John 4:3). John makes a distinct reference here to the *spirit of antichrist,* which he stated was already in the world.

John identifies this spirit as one that does not confess Jesus. To a first-century saint, to "confess Jesus" meant more than simply mentioning His name after a prayer. Essentially, it was to speak from a state of oneness with Him, enabling His actual Spirit to be manifest (see Matthew 10:32 AMP). They confessed the *Person* Jesus, not just the name "Jesus." Christ Himself was revealed through their attitudes of love, commitment, and sacrifice!

In the next verse John explained the nature of the antichrist spirit.

> By this we know the spirit of truth and the spirit of error. Beloved, *let us love one another*, for love is from God; and everyone who loves is born of God and knows God. The one who does not love does not know God, for God is love.   —1 John 4:6–8, italics mine

We discern the spirit of truth from the spirit of error—or more specifically, the Spirit of Christ from the spirit of antichrist—by the measure of Christ's love operating in an individual or church. John says that "the one who does not love does not know God." *An individual or church that thinks God is pleased with them, yet they do not walk in love, may actually be serving the spirit of antichrist.* Christians are to be known by their love, not merely their theology (see John 13:35). When John wrote of truth and error, he spoke specifically of the antichrist spirit and our openness to this spirit through loveless church attitudes.

This display of the antichrist is far more subtle and much more subversive than what may take place when the "man of sin" (2 Thessalonians 2:3) is openly revealed. The antichrist spirit hardens the heart, keeping it from love. It nurtures unforgiving attitudes, causing those under its influence to splinter from a church due to various criticisms and minor doctrinal differences. It is the "strong man" behind most church splits.

Following Christ, however, calls us to embrace forgiveness and love as a way of life. It is simply "anti" Christ to justify unforgiveness, division and selfish ambition. *The antichrist spirit will be disguised behind any number of issues, but those issues are simply tools this principality uses to divide the church.*

The spirit of antichrist is simply that spirit which is anti-Christ. It is anti-love, anti-forgiveness, anti-reconciliation. Perhaps more than all others, this principality keeps good churches divided from one another.

Antichrist is the true source of numerous church splits. Indeed, if you pray against this spirit instead of what seems like the immediate issues, many church splits would be averted. In this sense, we must guard very carefully how strongly we cling to our ideas and criticisms. For if our thoughts exalt themselves above God's ability to correct us, we will certainly become a target for the spirit of antichrist. Remember, the antichrist spirit may use jealousy or fear or even the color of the church bathrooms as a smoke screen, but the essential cause of most division is simply Christians yielding to someone or something other than the Spirit and teachings of Jesus Christ. Any situation can be reconciled by returning to the words of Jesus. Once all parties agree to yield to Him, love and victory soon follow.

DELIVERANCE FROM ANTICHRIST ON A PERSONAL LEVEL

Each of us has thinking processes, strongholds in our minds, which have been shaped and conditioned by the spirit of antichrist. Let us not defend those thoughts or attitudes that are "anti" Christ; rather, let us expose them as sin and see them defeated. Antichrist has been around for a long time; its thought-systems may not depart suddenly from any of us. But if we can discern the difference between the loving voice of Christ and the arrogant rebellion of antichrist, we can take a major step toward seeing our lives conformed to our Savior.

How do you know if the lack of love you feel toward other churches is only your flesh or if it is a stronghold for the spirit of antichrist? Repent for rebellion and cold love. Ask God to give you His love for all those who are truly born again. Then audibly pray against the antichrist spirit. You will immediately discover a distance between you and the enemy and a closeness between you and the Lord.

CHRISTIANITY WITHOUT THE ANTICHRIST INFLUENCE

There are many ways the antichrist spirit seeks to display itself as being God: the New Age Movement, Communism, etc. But the unique way it masquerades in the church as God is this: there is a natural, religious reverence men have toward death. Antichrist uses this phenomenon by conditioning congregations to accept the solemnity of death as though it were true reverence of God. The Almighty, however, is not the God of the dead but of the living, and true reverence is that which is accompanied by awe, joy and thanksgiving.

You can discern antichrist in a congregation that is reverent toward its deadness. The atmosphere is not filled with holiness but hollowness. *It is the same essence that lingers in an empty funeral home.* Antichrist will sit over a people, exuding an aura of coldness that literally fills the atmosphere of a church building.

When the Holy Spirit first began to unveil this entity, we saw how it had distorted our basic concept of Christianity. In fact, the stronghold of antichrist thinking is an "acceptable" condition in the church. This spirit has so worked its way into "the temple of God" (the corporate but divided city-church), that in many congregations and to many believers, it is "displaying [itself] as being God" (2 Thessalonians 2:4).

It was obvious to us that this principality was seeking to "exalt [itself] above all that is called God" (NKJV). When we sought to teach the people, the words of our messages fell to the ground amidst tremendous resistance, as though a blanket were covering them. We sought the Lord and a few days later the Holy Spirit revealed the discernment we had been missing. He illuminated the first words of 2 Thessalonians 2:4, "[he] opposes."

The antichrist spirit literally *opposes* truth, especially new truth that unmasks its nature. It resists any movement in the body of Christ toward life. In the churches where it presides, should an "amen" squeak out of one in support of the preaching, this spirit glares through the faces of those whose minds are its stronghold.

When we better understood the antichrist spirit, we could war successfully against it. Our intercessors began to pray against this spirit's influence over our county. Less than one week later, five other pastors and myself, as well as several para-church ministries, gathered together and committed ourselves to meet for weekly intercessory prayer in each other's churches. Three months later, that number had doubled and has been increasing ever since. How did it occur? The intercessors discerned and bound the spirit of antichrist. Suddenly the godly desires to meet and pray with other pastors began to prevail in our community!

UNDERSTANDING THE CITYWIDE CHURCH

God sees the church community as one body fused together in the fire of Christ's love. He would have us praying together, working and building our churches in the spirit of His kingdom. No one knows the local battle better than the local pastors. When Jesus spoke to the churches in the Revelation of John, He identified the church as a local organism in each city. He did not say, "To the Christians in Asia who are of Paul, I say this . . ."

No. Jesus addressed the churches by the name of their geographic locations. They may have had spiritual roots with extra-local apostolic leaders, but their primary relationships were with each other (see Acts 13:1–2). These were local people who knew the people's needs, and Jesus viewed them as such.

Yet, the penetration of the antichrist spirit into typical Christian thinking is so deep that its deceptions are preached from pulpits and accepted in the pews. Therefore, you must persevere for the sake of Christ in your community.

Let your faith continually increase while your fleshly ambitions proportionally decrease. Personal ambition is the motive of the antichrist; it is the name of the stronghold that has made us divided. You must approach others in the spirit of servanthood, not with the motive of fulfilling selfish ambition. If you are called to a leadership role, the others will recognize that call by your meekness and good fruit. Your ministry will come naturally, without self-promotion. Remember the commandment of Jesus: "Do not be called leaders; for One is your Leader, that is, Christ" (Matthew 23:10). In truth, God is not raising up leaders; He is training bond-servants, men and women who will pray together for Christ's leading.

Therefore, when you meet with Christians from other churches, come as their servant and look to bless them. If you are a pastor, find out the needs of your fellow pastors and begin to pray for them. Perhaps one needs a piano player; if you have two, send a pianist (see Luke 3:11). Most pastors struggle with unique fears and insecurities. But if you come in the love of God, you will disarm their fears.

The spirit of antichrist is a world ruler (see Ephesians 6:12). It cannot be cast out as a lesser demon might. Ultimate victory over all such principalities comes through *displacement,* where the encouragement and love of Christ floods the thought-life of the local Christian community. As we become the opposite of antichrist, we will see Christ's body healed, and the spirit of antichrist trodden under our feet.

CHAPTER 17

DISCERNING THE SPIRIT OF JEZEBEL

We are going to confront a stronghold of immense propor-
tions. It is a way of thinking that exists unchecked in most
churches. We are going to expose and then destroy the hiding
places of Jezebel.

UNDERSTANDING THE SPIRIT OF JEZEBEL

But I have this against you, that you tolerate the woman
Jezebel, who calls herself a prophetess, and she teaches
and leads My bond-servants astray, so that they commit
acts of immorality and eat things sacrificed to idols.

—Revelation 2:20

You may challenge addressing the above quote to American
churches. You may argue that not one of the pastors you know
has anyone who openly instructs people to commit acts of

immorality. I understand your sense of alarm. I agree that you probably know of no one who brazenly preaches that sexual lust and idolatry are not sins. When we speak of Jezebel, we are identifying the source in our society of obsessive sensuality, unbridled witchcraft, and hatred for male authority.

To understand the spirit of Jezebel, we must understand the genesis of this personality in the Bible. The first mention of Jezebel is seen in the rebellious, manipulative wife of King Ahab. It was actually this spirit, operating through Queen Jezebel, which had caused millions of Israelites from the northern ten tribes—all but seven thousand faithful souls—to bow to Baal. Under her control, these people had forsaken the covenant, destroyed the sacred altars, and killed the prophets (see 1 Kings 19:14–18). Think of it! This one spirit was almost totally responsible for corrupting an entire nation. And it is this principality that today has come full force against our nation.

Jezebel is fiercely independent and intensely ambitious for pre-eminence and control. Jezebel will not dwell with anyone unless she can control and dominate the relationship. When she seems submissive or servant-like, it is only for the sake of gaining some strategic advantage. From her heart, she yields to no one.

Bear in mind that the spirit which produced Jezebel existed before its namesake was born. Although we refer to Jezebel as "she," this spirit is without gender. However, it is important to note that Jezebel is more attracted to the uniqueness of the female psyche in its sophisticated ability to manipulate without physical force.

Look for Jezebel to target women who are embittered against men either through neglect or misuse of authority. This spirit operates through women who, because of insecurity, jealousy or vanity, desire to control and dominate others. Jezebel is behind the woman who publicly humiliates her husband with her tongue and then thereafter controls him by his fear of public embarrassment.

While she uses every means of sexual perversity known in hell, immorality is not the issue; *control* is what she seeks, using the power of sexual passions for the purpose of possessing men. To a woman under the influence of Jezebel, "conquering" a man need not involve physical contact if a seductive glance of her eyes will capture him.

THE BATTLE HAS EXPANDED

Since the era of the early apostles, and especially since the dawn of the electronic age, the scale of battle has greatly enlarged. It is difficult for us in our generation to discern the scope of warfare that hits the church and the world in general. We might actually suppose that warfare should decrease since the number of demons has not changed since the first century, while mankind has grown from 150 million in the apostolic age to more than six billion souls today. Yet, the *access* the devil has to the souls in our world has increased through the mass communications media and literature. John wrote of this period in time in Revelations 12:15: "And the serpent poured water like a river out of his mouth after the woman, so that he might cause her [the church] to be swept away with the flood."

Water, in this context, symbolizes "words." In our world there exists a flood of *words* and *visual images* coming out of the mouth of Satan. Our society, through technological advances, has made sins of the mind and heart more accessible. More than ever before, the carnal mind, with its openness to this satanic flood of filth and rebellion, is being structured into a powerful stronghold for the devil.

In our information-filled, entertainment-oriented world, even minor demons can exercise major influence simply by possessing the script writers and producers of movies and television. Indeed, Satan has always been "the prince of the power of the air" (Ephesians 2:2). But we should realize that the "power of the air" is not merely the wind; we see that in our world this power uniquely includes the electronic airwaves which carry radio and television signals.

Therefore, we must discern exactly where the satanic inroads are in our own lives and cut them off. We cannot worship God Sunday morning and then tolerate Jezebel through immoral entertainment in a movie Sunday night. Indeed, it is with this in mind that, in regard to warring against Jezebel, Jesus described Himself as "He who searches the *minds* and *hearts*" (Revelation 2:23, italics mine). For it is in the inner sanctuary of our soul life where tolerance to Jezebel begins. It is here, within us, where tolerance must end.

SET THE CAPTIVES FREE!

Jezebel's spirit flows unhindered throughout the entertainment industries. It flaunts itself in the world of fashion; it holds degrees in the philosophical departments of our schools and colleges. Where can you go in our society that the influence of this spirit is not felt? She is the destroyer of politician and preacher alike. She is the cruel motivator behind abortion. It is Jezebel who frequently generates dissatisfaction between spouses.

This spirit was sitting in the church in Thyatira when the Holy Spirit exposed it nineteen hundred years ago (see Revelation 2:19–29). It still has its favorite seat in church today. There are respectable men who love God and who seek to serve Him, yet secretly in their hearts they are prisoners of Jezebel. Even now, they are deeply ashamed of their bondage to pornography, and they can barely control their desires for women. Ask them to pray and their spirits are awash with guilt and shame. Their prayers are but the whimpers of Jezebel's eunuchs.

There are good women who come to church seeking God, but this spirit has them fantasizing about the men in their assembly—lamenting that their husbands are not as "spiritual" as other husbands. Soon, these women develop problems that "only the pastor" can understand. Ladies, the "older women" (Titus 2:3–5)—the *godly* women in the church—are the ones you need to consult with first, not the pastor or elders. If you must counsel with a church leader, do not be offended when he asks for his wife or an older, godly woman to join him.

Anyone who is hit by this spirit needs, first of all, to repent deeply of their sympathetic thoughts toward it, and then *war* against it! Do not waste days and weeks under condemnation. Separate yourself from that Jezebelian thinking that was fostered upon you in your youth, pick up the sword of the Spirit, and war against the spirit of Jezebel! Pray for the saints in your church. Pray for the Christians throughout your community. *If you war against Jezebel when you are tempted, eventually you are going to become dangerous.* This spirit will stop attacking you once it recognizes that your aggressive counterattack is setting other people free.

LIKELY TARGETS

We have stated that this spirit prefers to exploit the more complex nature of a woman, yet this demon can also operate through men. In fact, Jezebel seeks the highly refined qualities of the professional musician, especially when such a man has both the ambition and the opportunity to become a worship leader or director. It will also seek to surface in the life of the pastor himself, in which case he will become very authoritarian and unyielding in his control of the church. Such a pastor will invariably be isolated from fellowship and accountability with other pastors. The man will find himself lured into maintaining flirtatious and sensual relationships, "special intimacies" with one or more women in the church. In time, he will most likely succumb to adultery.

Yet this spirit more often seeks the disposition of the feminine nature. And since certain female ministries are more involved than others, it follows that they could become targets for the spirit of Jezebel. Church leaders should take heed. This spirit will seek to maneuver itself into leadership positions. Remember, Jesus said of Jezebel, "[she] calls herself a prophetess" (Revelation 2:20). A woman can most certainly function prophetically; she can be anointed by God to serve in delegated authority as a prophetess. But when she insists upon recognition, when she manipulates or entirely disregards the male leadership in the church, when she "calls herself a prophetess," beware.

Prayer leaders, church secretaries, worship and song leaders, pastors and their spouses, you are all especially targeted by this spirit. All of you serving in these roles should be instructed and warned about the warfare that may come against you. Each of you should be part of a church warfare team that is trained to discern and war against Jezebel.

WHAT JEZEBEL HATES

Jezebel hates repentance. Her worst fear is that the people will begin to mourn over their sins. Though this spirit will infiltrate the church, masking its desire for control with true Christian doctrines, it will hide from true repentance.

Jezebel hates humility. Jesus taught that greatness in the kingdom was measured in childlike honesty of heart, not in what we appear to be to others. *A true ministry is willing and eager to be submitted and accountable to other ministries.* It is typical of those who are servant-minded. Therefore, we must learn that spirituality is measured in meekness, not intellectual power.

Jezebel hates prayer. Intercessory prayer pries her fingers off the hearts and souls of men. It sets people free in the spirit. When you pray, it binds her. When you pray against immorality, it cripples her. When you pray for a submissive heart, it is like the trampling of Jehu's horse upon her body.

Jezebel hates the prophets, for the prophets speak out against her. The prophets are her worst enemies. When she wars, it is to stir people against the message of the prophetic church. Yet, more than her hatred for the prophet ministry, she hates the Word they speak. Her real enemy is the spoken Word of God.

Jezebel's ultimate hatred is against God Himself. She hates the grace God lavishes upon His bond-servants, even after they sin. She hates the fact that God will take the weakest and lowliest and use them to bring her down. She hates the holiness and purity of heart that comes from God and surrounds those who serve in His courts.

Let's pray: *Father, we submit to You and Your standard of righteousness. We ask for purity, meekness and holiness of heart. Forgive us for our tolerance of the spirit of Jezebel in both our mind and our deeds.*

Father, because we submit to You, we have Your authority to resist the devil. We bind, in the name of Jesus, the spirit of Jezebel. We pray against the stronghold of Jezebelic-thinking over our community and our state. We come against the fortresses this demon has built up in the spirit realm in this area and we ask the Holy Spirit to plunder the house of Jezebel and distribute her goods.

We also pray for faithfulness of eyes and heart to husbands and wives. We release purity of heart and grace to each member of the body of Christ, both single and married. We cover Your people with the blood of Jesus. We loose the joy of a humble and submissive spirit and pull down the imaginations of ambition and pride. In Jesus' name. Amen!

CHAPTER 18

ELIJAH, JEHU, AND THE WAR AGAINST JEZEBEL

There is a war, a very ancient war, between the spirit of Elijah and the spirit of Jezebel. In this age-old battle, Elijah represents the interests of heaven: the call to repentance and the return to God. Jezebel, on the other hand, represents that unique principality whose purpose is to hinder and defeat the work of repentance.

TO THE VICTOR GOES OUR NATION

To understand the conflict between the Elijah spirit and the spirit of Jezebel, we must understand these two adversaries as they are seen in the Scriptures. Each is the spiritual counterpart of the other. Is Elijah bold? Jezebel is brazen. Is Elijah ruthless toward evil? Jezebel is vicious toward righteousness. Does Elijah speak of the ways and words of God? Jezebel is full of systems of witchcraft and words of deceit. The war between Elijah and Jezebel continues today. The chief warriors on either side are the prophets of both foes; to the victor goes the soul of our nation.

In the tradition of Samuel, Elijah was the head of the school of prophets. Under him were the sons of the prophets—literally hundreds of seers and prophetic minstrels—who proclaimed the Word of the Lord. In this war, however, Jezebel had viciously and systematically murdered all of God's servants until only Elijah remained (see 1 Kings 18:22). Elijah, as the last of the prophets, then challenged the 450 prophets of Baal and the 400 prophets of the Asherah to a demonstration of power: their gods against the power of the Lord.

These 850 men were the false prophets, the satanic priests "who ate at Jezebel's table" (1 Kings 18:19). They were the most powerful, demonized individuals that the hosts of darkness could produce. King Ahab, Jezebel's husband, sent a message out to "all the sons of Israel" (v. 20), and the nation came to witness the war between the God of Elijah and the demons of Jezebel.

The terms of the challenge were simple: each was to place an ox upon an altar. Elijah then said, "You call on the name of your god, and I will call on the name of the Lord, and the God who answers by fire, He is God" (v. 24). Six hours later the cult priests still could produce no fire; twelve hours passed and Elijah began to mock them, "Call out [to Baal] with a loud voice, for he is a god; either he is occupied or gone aside . . . perhaps he is asleep and needs to be awakened" (v. 27). Then, just before evening, Elijah prayed over his sacrifice and "the fire of the Lord fell, and consumed the burnt offering." The

Scriptures continue: "When all the people saw it, they fell on their faces; and they said, 'The Lord, He is God; the Lord, He is God' " (vv. 38–39). Immediately after this powerful witness of the Lord, Elijah had the Hebrews secure the prophets of Baal and all of them were put to death.

We would suppose that, at this point, Elijah would have gone into Jezreel and asked God to finish off Jezebel, but he did not. In fact—and this may surprise you—Elijah came under spiritual warfare. When Jezebel heard what had happened to her servants, in a fit of rage she released a flood of witchcraft and demonic power against Elijah that put fear into his heart, and Elijah fled.

You may ask, "How could such a mighty prophet turn and run?" The answer is not simple. In fact, the situation worsened. We then see Elijah sitting under a juniper tree, bewailing that he is no better than his fathers—actually praying that he might die! (see 1 Kings 19:4) What pressure overwhelmed this great man of God that he would fall prey to fear and discouragement? He succumbed to the witchcraft of Jezebel.

And now, let the reader understand. *When you stand against the principality of Jezebel, even though you resist her lusts and witchcrafts, you must guard against the power-demons of fear and discouragement, for these she will send against you to distract you from your warfare and your victory!*

THE DRAMA CONTINUES . . .

It is a mystery, yet biblically true, that under certain conditions the Holy Spirit will transfer a leader's anointing to one or more uniquely prepared people. This occurred when the Lord took the "Spirit who was upon [Moses], and placed the same upon the seventy elders" (Numbers 11:24–25 NKJV). Again, we see the effect of this principle with Joshua, who "was filled with the spirit of wisdom, for Moses had laid his hands on him" (Deuteronomy 34:9). Of course, our very salvation reaps the reward of this precept, for Christ is not just a religion to us, but His actual Spirit and virtue have been imparted to us.

With this concept in mind, we can better accept how the spirit of Elijah was sent to minister through the person of John the Baptist. Once before, Elijah's spirit had been placed upon another individual. You will remember that Elisha, the prophet who succeeded Elijah, received a double portion of Elijah's spirit (see 2 Kings 2:9–11). Now, again, the spirit of Elijah was ministering, activating, inspiring and creating in John the Baptist that same kind of intensity which dwelt in Elijah himself. John was to go "as a forerunner before [the Lord] in the spirit and power of Elijah" (Luke 1:17).

Jesus said of the Baptist, "John himself is Elijah who was to come" (Matthew 11:14, see also 17:11–13). John even *looked* like Elijah. The spiritual influence of Elijah had returned to the world in the person of John the Baptist. Like Elijah, John proclaimed the need for repentance wherever he saw sin. One such area was in the adulterous lives of King Herod and his wife Herodias. When John confronted them, Herodias had him imprisoned (see Mark 6:17–18).

But who was this manipulating and working through the dark, psychic side of Herodias? As Elijah's spirit ministered through John, so *Jezebel* had resurfaced through the rebellion of the seductress, Herodius. Remember, through Jezebel's many witchcrafts (see 2 Kings 9:22), she attacked Elijah, causing *fear* and *discouragement*, which led to Elijah's time of self-doubt and confusion. Now Herodius had come forcibly against the Baptist. This is the prophet who had visibly seen the Spirit descend upon Christ; he heard the Father's audible voice announcing His beloved Son; he gazed with awe upon the purity of Israel's Messiah. Now, fear and discouragement are weighing upon the prophet's shoulders. Doubt floods his soul about Christ: "Are You the Expected One, or shall we look for someone else?" (Matthew 11:3).

"A strategic day came when Herod . . . gave a banquet" (Mark 6:21). "Strategic" is the perfect word to describe the timing of this event. For in this war between the spirits of Elijah and Jezebel, Herodias had her daughter dance before Herod, enticing out of him a promise to give whatever she asked. At her mother's request—more truly, at *Jezebel's* request—she demanded and received the head of the Baptist. And temporarily, the confrontation between the spirits of these two eternal enemies subsided.

ELIJAH IS COMING!

Two thousand years ago, Jesus stated that the ministry of Elijah was not over. He promised, "Elijah is coming and will restore all things" (Matthew 17:11). Also, Malachi the prophet wrote, "Behold, I am going to send you Elijah the prophet before the coming of the great and terrible day of the Lord. He will restore . . ." (Malachi 4:5–6). Elijah is coming to war and restore. He came before the great day and he is returning before the terrible day of the Lord.

Remember, however, the principle of impartation. *For today, even as God did with Elijah, Elisha and John the Baptist, the Lord is raising up an Elijah company of prophets, Spirit-filled men and women sent forth to prepare the way for the return of Christ!*

Let it also be known that if Elijah is coming before Jesus returns, so also is Jezebel. Indeed, do you not see her in our land in the abundance of witchcraft and harlotries? Do you not hear her brazen voice rejecting God's authority and exalting her rebellion in radical feminism? Have you not, with shame, beheld her as she caused God's "bond-servants" to "commit acts of immorality" (Revelation 2:20)? Seeing Jezebel so blatantly manifest herself only confirms that the spirit of Elijah is also here bringing repentance and raising up warring prophets throughout our land. In fact, if you are going to serve God during the reign of a "Jezebel," the warfare itself will thrust you into a prophetic anointing simply that you may survive!

In the Old Testament we see how God destroyed Jezebel. Jehu, the newly crowned king of Israel, was sent by the word of the Lord through Elijah's successor, Elisha, to fulfill God's promise. As Jehu and his men furiously drove their chariots toward Jezreel, the kings of Israel and Judah came out to meet him. They asked, "Is it peace, Jehu?" And he answered, "What peace, so long as the harlotries of your mother Jezebel and her witchcrafts are so many?" (2 Kings 9:21–22) And Jehu slew the two kings. Immediately afterward, he rode into Jezreel to confront Jezebel. The Word tells us that when she saw him,

> She painted her eyes and adorned her head (v. 30) and looking out an upper window, she called to him, "Is it well, Zimri, your master's murderer?" Then he lifted up his face to the window and said, "Who is on my side? Who?" And two or three officials looked down at him. He said, "Throw her down." So they threw her down, and some of her blood was sprinkled on the wall and on the horses, and he trampled her under foot.
>
> —2 Kings 9:31–33

There was something in Jehu's spirit that we must possess today. While we must be compassionate toward those captured by her influence (see Revelation 2:21), we must show no mercy to the Jezebel spirit itself. Jehu offered Jezebel no hope for reform, no compromise whatsoever. So we must offer this demon no opportunity to probe our soul and unlock vulnerabilities to her "many witchcrafts." She must be cast down from her high place of influence. Indeed, as she lay bleeding and near death, Jehu "trampled her underfoot!" Likewise, we must follow Christ and fearlessly walk upon this serpent, crushing it under our feet (see Luke 10:19; Romans 16:20).

So also with us, we must have no tolerance whatsoever for this spirit. *There can be no peace, no relaxing under our "fig tree" until the spirit of Jezebel is conquered!* We must stop living for comfort as long as her harlotries and witchcrafts are so many in our land. We must refuse to settle for a false peace based on compromise and fear, especially when the Spirit of God is calling for war!

It is significant that the *eunuchs* cast her down. Some of you who are reading this have been made eunuchs, slaves to this evil spirit. Today, right now, God is giving you the privilege of participating in the eternal judgment against Jezebel. *You* cast her down! Side with God, and let the judgments of God come forth.

It is time for the prophets to unite against this spirit. Even now, we wash ourselves in the precious blood of Jesus. Under the anointing of Elijah, in the power of the Holy Spirit, let us arise in the indignation of Jehu and cast Jezebel down!

Pray with me: *Heavenly Father, I submit my heart to You. In the name and authority of Jesus Christ, I turn now against the spirit of Jezebel. As a servant of Jesus Christ, I release those who have been Jezebel's captives, even those reading*

CHAPTER **19**

OUR EXPERIENCE
WITH JEZEBEL

What we present to you comes from our experience. We offer you no theories, no speculations. What we share with you has worked.

TO DELIVER, WE OURSELVES
MUST BE DELIVERED

"He will deliver one who is not innocent, and he will be delivered through the cleanness of your hands" (Job 22:30). There is a difference between repenting for a sin and actually pulling down the stronghold within us that produced the sin. The first involves faith in the cross of Christ; the second demands we embrace crucifixion ourselves. In this regard, in 1971 the Lord began a foundational work of cleansing my heart from the influence of the Jezebel spirit.

This season of repentance lasted about forty days. During that time, through the Holy Spirit, the stronghold which was tolerant toward the spirit of Jezebel was pulled down. I should make it clear that I was not repenting again for sins previously washed and forgiven. My repentance was not for sin but for the *nature* that caused my sins. This is the essence of pulling down strongholds: we destroy the defiling, oppressive *system of thinking* which, through the years, has been structured into our nature. My goal was simply that I "be renewed in the spirit of [my] mind" (Ephesians 4:23).

The manner in which this happened was as follows: the Holy Spirit brought to mind many of the sins from my unsaved youth. Two or three times a day, every day, in dreams or as I worked, the Lord brought events to my mind. As the Lord revealed these incidents, I covered each memory with the blood of Jesus. Each time I prayed, I knew that through the Spirit another "stone" was being removed from this fortress in my mind.

Finally, the Lord revealed through a dream that this stronghold had been pulled down. In the dream two men were talking, one of whom was holding a baby. The one holding the child used a vile word in his conversation. Suddenly embarrassed because of the infant, he quickly reassured himself that the baby was so innocent that it did not know the meaning of the immoral word. In the dream, I realized that I also did not know the meaning of this word. In this, the grace of God had brought a new innocence into my heart of which the baby in the dream was a symbol. At that time I knew nothing of the spirit of Jezebel. Nevertheless, the Lord was building in me a measure of immunity against it.

OUR FIRST ENCOUNTER WITH JEZEBEL

During the 1970s I pastored in an organization that had a number of leaders who functioned in the revelation gifts. There was "day and night" prayer, beautiful worship, commitment and power. As the Lord was to the nation of Israel on the plains of Moab, so He was also to us like the horns of the wild ox (see Numbers 22–25). There seemed to be no curse or omen that worked against us; God had given us His blessing; success seemed inevitable. But as Balaam counseled Balak to seduce the Israelites with the daughters of Moab, so the spirit of Jezebel launched its attack upon this work of God.

If the enemy cannot attack you directly, he will seek to bring you into sin, thereby positioning you under the judgments of God. When the Jezebel spirit began to manifest itself, and tolerance toward sexual sins increased, I approached the founder of the movement with my concerns. Meeting with him privately, I entreated him as a son does a father, but he dismissed me. Three months later I approached him again, appealing this time to the entire governmental team that was with him, warning them with tears that the judgment of the Lord against tolerating Jezebel was sickness and death (Revelation 2:22–23). Once more I was dismissed. Several months later I was taken out of leadership and then, ultimately, the hand of the Lord removed me from the group. Within months after I left, the leader divorced his wife, and less than a year later he married his secretary. Within two years he was dead from prostate cancer.

The impact of this experience was both devastating and enlightening. Even though I personally went through a period of great discouragement and self-doubt, I learned much about Jezebel and the sin of presumption. I saw that when men assume

God will not judge or punish them for their sin, it is only a matter of time before the tempter comes to destroy them. It is significant that, while Jesus had the spirits of wisdom and understanding, counsel, strength and knowledge, His *delight* was "in the fear of the Lord" (Isaiah 11:2–3). The sin of presumption is the antithesis of the fear of the Lord. It is the harbinger of future defeat.

RELEASING SOULS THROUGH PRAYER

That was our first experience with the spirit of Jezebel, though not the last. In 1985, during a time of counseling, we discerned that this spirit was the controlling influence directing the lesser demons of homosexuality and lesbianism. The Lord instructed us to war against Jezebel, and in one month's time three people were delivered from these perversions. The next month the local cable network removed the Playboy channel. People began calling for help with sexual problems and needing deliverance from fantasies. Even a couple of pastors and their wives discreetly called, feeling compelled to confess their sins in search of deliverance. By focusing our warfare against the Jezebel spirit, many in her grip were being set free.

At the same time, the warfare suddenly increased against both my family and our church. A faultfinding demon (which we had not discerned until months later) brought division and conflict into the congregation. Certain people whom we loved deeply suddenly turned against us with unexplained hatred. Suspicion mounted in the church and a time of destabilization occurred. Nevertheless, we continued warring against the spirit of Jezebel, convinced our warfare was effective.

One night, however, this same spirit of Jezebel appeared at the foot of our bed. I felt paralyzed, unable to speak or even cry for help. This spirit was now manifest before me in a dark spirit form. All my natural life seemed literally drained from my body. I felt that only Christ's life sustained me.

No audible words were spoken, but I suddenly heard the following words in my mind, *"Continue to pray as you are and I will kill you and the members of your church."* The spirit faded, but even after it had apparently left, I was barely able to move. My mind was a quagmire of discouraging thoughts: "Why should I pray for these people? Why suffer when, on any given day, I don't know who will be turned against me?" Fortunately, the Holy Spirit intervened and lifted me from my oppression.

But Jezebel's death threat was not idle. A few days later, on a Saturday night, a woman in our church called, frantic for help. Her husband had taken narcotics and was threatening her and her children. We made provisions for her, and she and her children escaped to a home in our neighborhood. At 1:00 a.m. that same night, I received a phone call from her enraged husband. This man, a self-styled Nazi and owner of thirty-four guns, was demanding I tell him where his wife was. He said, "If you don't tell me where my wife is, *I will kill you and the members of your church!*" These were the exact words the spirit of Jezebel had used in my bedroom less than one week earlier! It was obvious that the Jezebel spirit had found and raised up a vessel to carry out the death threat of the previous week.

It is not normal practice for pastors to pray *for* a snowstorm on a Saturday night, but we prayed that night and the light snow falling outside turned into a blizzard, dropping 10 inches of snow by church time Sunday morning. Those of us at church prayed again and bound Jezebel from the man who had threatened us. Eventually, to God's glory, this individual accepted the Lord Jesus as his Savior.

This has been a brief summary of our experience with the spirit of Jezebel. What we have written is not based upon theory or conjecture but experience. Our testimony in this warfare is simply this: the Lord Jesus Himself has given us His authority "over *all* the power of the enemy." His promise is faithful: *"and nothing will injure you"* (Luke 10:19, italics mine).

CHAPTER **20**

STRATEGY AGAINST THE SPIRIT OF JEZEBEL

You cannot defeat the enemy simply with prayer. To topple Satan's empire we must be transformed into Christ's likeness.

OUR WAR AGAINST JEZEBEL

The church that successfully wars against Jezebel will be a church that inherits the glorious "morning star" (Revelation 2:28), which will be a visible outward glory, a symbol of hidden, inward purity. It will be a church that ultimately exercises "authority over the nations" (v. 26), uniquely because it has conquered the Jezebel spirit which sought to strip the church of authority. It will be a church in which the gift of healing is an integral part of their body ministry.

There are great prizes to winning the war against Jezebel. Although every victory is initiated by prayer, God's rewards will not be attained only through intercession. As we have stated: *Victory begins with the name of Jesus on our lips; it is not consummated until the nature of Jesus is in our hearts.*

Therefore, in regard to our war against Jezebel, we must allow the Holy Spirit to expose where we are tolerant and sympathetic to its ways. *We cannot be successful in the heavenly war if we are not victorious in the battlefield of our minds.* There is only one realm of final victory against the enemy: Christlikeness.

Jesus is He "who searches the minds and hearts" (Revelation 2:23). Our victory in every battle begins here, in our "minds and hearts." Consequently, we cannot tolerate Jezebelian thinking in any area. Our concept of church must expand beyond buildings into a way of life we practice everywhere. Since we are the church, let us realize that we are still in the church when we are home. When we turn on television to an immoral program or view a web site that is illicit, we are still in the church, tolerating the spirit of Jezebel.

If a husband is afraid of his strong-willed wife or unable to serve as the head of his household, although he is not in the worship building, he is still in the church tolerating Jezebel. Our time spent in the worship service is necessary, but it is a very small part of our continuing church-life. It is in our daily, routine living where the strongholds of Jezebel must be confronted and destroyed.

IT TAKES AN "AHAB" TO TOLERATE JEZEBEL

There is a spirit that works alongside Jezebel. The effect of this demon is that it floods the soul of a man with weakness and fear. Its name is Ahab; his nature is *one who gives his authority to Jezebel.*

The Ahab spirit occupies the areas of tolerance within a man's mind. The man feels almost drugged in his struggle against Jezebel. To win against Jezebel, one must conquer the nature of Ahab.

The essence of Ahab is a title, "husband," and a position, "head," but the man has no real authority. When Ahab was king, Jezebel ruled. The man who cannot govern his household with godly, loving and protective authority will not exercise his spiritual authority elsewhere. Such a man needs to repent of his fears and firmly, with gentleness and patience, set his home in order.

But let us further clarify authority. Authority is simply delegated responsibility. The emphasis is not on being the boss but being responsible. The substructure upon which divine authority comes forth is divine love. Headship in the home is simply the man taking loving responsibility for the condition of his family. No man will have peace in his home if he views authority as simply the domination of his wife. God would have couples making decisions together, each drawing upon the wisdom of the other, enjoying themselves as friends in open and loving communion. God's answer to dealing with Jezebel is not to exchange one form of oppression (Jezebel's) for another (the man's). Our objective is to replace Jezebel's concept of security with the security a woman receives when she is tenderly loved by her husband. Thus, the man wins the war against Jezebel by becoming Christlike.

The woman overcomes the haughtiness of Jezebel by seeking the meekness of Christ. She pursues a "gentle and quiet spirit" (see 1 Peter 2:23–3:4), which is natural to Christlikeness. The woman must see God's wisdom in the divine order of the family and honor her husband as her head. If she is unmarried, she should be submitted to the order God has established in her church as unto the Lord. Her humility and peace in serving others is a sign of destruction to the nature of Jezebel (see Philippians 1:28).

The woman conquers the sensual side of Jezebel by renouncing her feminine charms, which are "deceitful" (Proverbs 31:30), and her "many persuasions" (Proverbs 7:21), which are enticing. She refuses the sensual look of the eyes and seductive softening of the voice. If she is married, her beauty is given to her husband. If she is single, she adorns her inner person with the spiritual qualities of the fruit of the Spirit, knowing that if she compromises her standards with God, she will inevitably find a man who will compromise his standards with her. The true man God has for her is a godly man in search of a virtuous woman. Her victory begins with prayer, but it is consummated by transformation.

What we become in Christ, *as His people,* must be the exact opposite of the spirit of Jezebel. Is she rebellious? We must become submissive. Is she proud and haughty? We must become meek and lowly of heart. Is she a control demon? We must be gentle and willing to yield. Does Jezebel send forth witchcraft and immorality, fear and discouragement? We must live a crucified life in the purity of Christ, full of love and faith for our vision. Again, it is who Christ becomes in us that establishes our victory against the spirit of Jezebel.

CORPORATE WARFARE AGAINST SATAN'S POWERS

"They lifted their voices to God with one accord" (Acts 4:24). As important as it is to win the war against Jezebel in the home, we must also join together for corporate prayer and warfare. Corporate warfare prayer is the united intercession of the church against the powers of darkness; the goal is to create greater freedom to win the lost and increased Christlikeness among the saved. The following precepts should be considered essential to effective warfare.

❑ Worship should be part of warfare. With great diversity of expression, worship and praise should be integrated into warfare. During our warfare, various individuals spontaneously will lead out with appropriate songs. Keep your eyes on Jesus and stay thankful!

❑ Intercession should be Spirit led. This is more than "praying in tongues." It requires we learn to listen. Often, corporate prayer is actually hindered by someone dominating the group with loud, insensitive "tongues." When you pray corporately, there is a *common fountain* from which those who pray must draw. It requires we be responsive to the subtle changes of the Spirit as He guides the group into creative agreement. As individuals, we seek to keep our prayers short (two to four minutes); we address one need at a time, leaving the door open for others to pray in agreement.

❑ Seek to remain consistent to scheduled prayer times. This may sound like we are seeking to control the Holy Spirit, but the more predictable the schedule, the more people can commit themselves to it. However, stay open for those special seasons when the Lord orders additional intercession.

❑ Do not become presumptuous. In fact, if someone resorts to calling the devil names, "daring him to fight," etc., instruct him that he is out of order. In prayer, use the Word, the Spirit, and the name of Jesus; anything more than these is fleshly.

❑ Keep all talk to a minimum. Save all but essential conversation for after prayer.

❑ Those who engage in warfare should be trained and approved by church leadership. In my opinion, it would be very helpful for churches to have a "warfare prayer team" which prays for those ministering on the front lines.

CHAPTER 21

DELIVERANCE FROM THE SPIRIT OF JEZEBEL

The Jezebel spirit is Satan's answer for a woman's protection in a harsh, male-dominated world.

GODLINESS OR WITCHCRAFT

The Jezebel spirit exploits the offenses a woman may have received from ungodly men, forcing the woman to utilize manipulation, sensuality and intimidation to make her way through life. Yet, it drives the woman beyond mere survival, developing her more intuitive nature until, whether she realizes it or not, the techniques she applies to personal relationships are akin to principles of witchcraft.

The entry of this spirit into the woman's life is full of irony. The woman, in her rebellion from the harsh, unloving demands of corrupt male authority, finds shelter and strength in becoming like her oppressor: she herself becomes harsh and unloving. Thus, the very thing she hated in men, she has now become.

The defense God offers for women, however, is the nature of Christ. Indeed, the antidote for the Jezebel spirit is Jesus' humility. His call to us requires that we crucify our "rights" and put our list of things which have offended us upon the cross. Thus, Christ makes all things new. Because we follow Him, we forgive those who have hurt us and love those who were our enemies. The effect of Christ's love not only offers hope for our antagonists but is a source of protection, a buffer between us and the harshness of life. Indeed, through the way of Christ we not only find protection but eternal life. We can become fruitful in the land of our affliction.

THE JOY OF SPIRITUAL FREEDOM

We know many women who once were in bondage to the Jezebel spirit but now have been delivered from its ways. These are women who function today in respected ministries throughout the nation. They do not feel they must become manlike to become ministries; they are feminine and glorify Christ in their womanhood, and they function in great authority and liberty.

The Jezebel spirit, however, is a perverse spirit which seeks to alter women into men and to make men into women. Since the Jezebel spirit offers an "illegal" strength to the woman, her deliverance will not begin until she can embrace a transition time of weakness. As Christ was crucified "because of weakness," yet He lives "because of the power of God" (2 Corinthians 13:4). So God will work dependency into the woman's heart until she trusts in the power and goodness of God for her security; she will renounce her ability to manipulate people.

The Jezebel stronghold is rooted in the woman's reactions to fear. She controls because she seeks predictability; she manipulates because she cannot trust. However, the Scriptures tell us that "perfect love casteth out fear: because fear hath torment" (1 John 4:18 KJV). During the process of deliverance, she needs godly men and women to stand with her in love, especially as she embraces the allotted times of weakness.

Remember, a woman under the influence of this spirit is a woman tormented. She has not been properly loved; the Jezebel stronghold is the result. Those who work to help such individuals should acknowledge with thankfulness that the woman who has come for help has already taken the first step toward her deliverance: *she recognizes her need.* You must confirm to her your commitment to this process of deliverance.

There are stages in deliverance. The deliverance of the soul is different than the liberation of a woman's spirit. The soul is made of life's events: the memories and hopes, loves and hates, experiences and reactions. It is your personality, intellect and emotions. Your spirit, however, is the silent observer when you dream; it is the evaluator of your thoughts. As it is written, "Who among men knows the thoughts of a man except the spirit of the man which is in him?" (1 Corinthians 2:11)

The human spirit is the "lamp of the Lord, searching all the innermost parts of his being" (Proverbs 20:27). Thus, it is in the woman's "innermost" being that she must recognize the difference between her hard, Jezebelian thoughts and the softness of Christ's way of life. She must identify in her spirit the subtle shift that moves her from trusting God to anxiously manipulating other people. Once she receives deliverance in her spirit from deception (see Psalm 32:2), she can proceed with deliverance in her soul.

The soul must experience renewal in the mind, that is, the full range of the individual's thought-life must be cleansed and retrained according to the Word of God. This process takes longer than the initial awakening of the individual's spirit and its subsequent deliverance.

In the process of the soul's deliverance, we should recognize that thoughts have their own survival instincts. No thought or idea graciously accepts death. Thus, our thoughts must be taken "captive to the obedience of Christ" (2 Corinthians 10:5), through which strongholds in the mind are pulled down.

The individual is well on the road to victory when, instead of becoming insecure when old Jezebel-like patterns emerge, she remains calm, even laughing at the way she used to react. She confidently abides in the peace and character of the Lord Jesus Christ.

CHAPTER 22

GOD WILL JUDGE YOUR JUDGMENT

The spirit of Babylon is the spirit of compromise with the world. Wherever there is compromise in our hearts with the devil, that compromise places us on the back of a beast that ultimately seeks our destruction.

IDENTIFYING THE SPIRIT OF BABYLON

The spirit of Babylon has been in the earth since civilization began. It is essential to understand this spirit if we desire to walk in God's kingdom without compromise, for the spirit of Babylon epitomizes self-exaltation, and self-exaltation is the source of compromise.

Originally, Babylon was more than a wealthy, glamorous city; it was primarily a religious city. To understand this gives us great insight into the nature of this enemy. Genesis 11:4 tells us that the common intent of its people was to build for themselves a city, "and a tower whose top will reach into heaven." More than their advanced skills in art and warfare, their pride was in their religion. When the Lord confused their tongues and scattered them across the earth, the spirit of Babylon spread throughout the world, and the desire to "reach into heaven" through man-made religions proliferated in every nation.

We also see in this spirit the ambition to "make for ourselves a name." As a result, this influence now permeates our human nature. Thus, Solomon observed, "every labor and every skill which is done is the result of rivalry between a man and his neighbor" (Ecclesiastes 4:4). Rivalry and the desire to make for oneself a name still comprise the nature of the spirit of Babylon.

One last thing about the origins of Babylon: the Scripture says the people journeyed east to the land of Shinar and "settled there" (Genesis 11:2). Any time a church stops pressing on and begins to "settle down," expect something Babylonian in nature to arise.

The influence of Babylonian philosophy is also seen in the book of Daniel. You will remember it was Babylon that conquered the Hebrews and carried them off into captivity. There Daniel was raised up to sit with the Chaldean wise men and conjurers who counseled King Nebuchadnezzar. We see this spirit in the thinking of the Babylonian priests when they were required to know what only the Almighty knew. They said, "The thing which the king demands is difficult, and there is no one else who could declare it to the king except gods, whose dwelling place is not with mortal flesh" (Daniel 2:11).

We can recognize the influence of Babylon in any people or church that offers lip service to a God far off, a deity whose dwelling place is not with men. In contrast, Jesus is our Emmanuel, "God with us." The very essence of true Christianity is Christ in us, the hope of glory. You can discern the spirit of Babylon in a church that honors God in heaven without having any relationship with Him on earth.

BABYLON WILL BE DESTROYED

The spirit of Babylon is all around us, both in our society in general and in the Christian church in particular. In the book of Revelation we see those who have compromised with this spirit. They are seen as "a woman sitting on a scarlet beast" (Revelation 17:3). Upon her forehead a name was written, "Babylon the Great, the mother of harlots" (v. 5).

To discern the spirit of Babylon, look first for pride: "Let us make for ourselves a name" (Genesis 11:4). Then, look for worldliness: "The woman was clothed in purple and scarlet, and adorned with gold and precious stones and pearls" (Revelation 17:4). Finally, where people are drunk with lusts for pleasure, you will see "in her hand a gold cup full of abominations and of the unclean things of her immorality" (v. 4).

The command of God is, "Come out of her, my people, so that you will not participate in her sins and receive of her plagues" (Revelation 18:4).

When we are called out of Babylon, it is a call into Christlikeness. In this hour God is certainly calling the church to enter into meekness, moderation, and purity of heart. The Holy Spirit has been judging and cleansing the Babylonian strongholds from the church. Indeed, the sins of Babylon will soon be fulfilled by plagues, which even now are falling upon her. In His mercy, God calls us out of this evil.

The Revelation of John continues, "The beast . . . will hate the harlot and will make her desolate and naked, and will eat her flesh and will burn her up with fire" (Revelation 17:16). Anytime we decide to coexist with the devil, it leaves us desolate and naked, suffering in unquenchable fire. This warning must be heard by each of us as individuals. In the sanctuary of our hearts, we must decide we are not going to compromise with Babylon in any way.

THOSE WHO CONQUER

At the same time, the Apocalypse speaks of a people who not only came out of Babylon, but under the Lord's direction they became instrumental in God's judgment of her. Concerning the fall of Babylon, Revelation 18:20 reads, literally, "Rejoice over her, O heaven, and you saints and apostles and prophets, because God has judged your judgment of her." John wrote here of saints, apostles and prophets in the last days whose words and whose purity became a source of judgment upon the spirit of Babylon. In fact, Scripture says that God will judge *their* judgment!

The Lord Jesus not only wants us separate from this spirit but to be warring against it. In other words, as we agree in spirit and character, in word and behavior, with the Word of God concerning righteousness, God will put in our mouths His judgments concerning evil. The simplicity and purity of our lives will be instrumental in exposing the powers of Babylon and releasing her prisoners.

We are not fighting flesh and blood but the powers of darkness that hold people captive. "Through the church" the manifold wisdom of God is made known "to the principalities and powers in the heavenly places" (Ephesians 3:10 NKJV).

Before Jesus returns, His church will be brought up to His standard in all aspects (see Ephesians 4:11–15). And that includes becoming an army that hates wickedness and loves righteousness, an army that, as it follows Christ, initiates spiritual warfare against the various gates of hell.

JESUS: OUR WARRIOR KING

Jesus is not returning as the "meek and mild" Lamb whom the world crucified. No, He is not coming again to be humiliated. He is returning "to be glorified in His saints . . . and to be marveled at among all who have believed" (2 Thessalonians 1:10). Within His saints first, He shall establish His rule in glory and be revealed in power (see Revelation 2:26; Jude 1:14–15). He is returning as the King of Kings and the Lord of Lords. This Lamb returns to earth treading "the wine press of the fierce wrath of God" (Revelation 19:15).

Speaking through the prophet, the Holy Spirit says, "The Lord will go forth like a warrior, He will arouse His zeal like a man of war. He will utter a shout, yes, He will raise a war cry. He will prevail against His enemies" (Isaiah 42:13). Do you hear the war cry our King is raising? It is the call to put away the idols of Babylon and approach the hour of our destiny with zeal and willing obedience to Jesus. As it is written, "Your people will volunteer freely in the day of Your power" (Psalm 110:3). Especially as we approach the end of this age, it is essential we understand that God's purpose is to conform us to the image of His Son. We are to grow up "in all aspects" of the Holy One, even into His likeness as Captain of the Hosts!

As you enter into the administration of the victory of Jesus Christ, what was once a walk filled with blindness and darkness will now become a walk of vision and light. Your words will declare God's purpose, and His purpose will empower your words. You will rejoice as you see the Spirit of God "judge your judgment" of Babylon.

Heavenly Father, we worship You. We declare that Your name shall be exalted in all the earth, even the name You gave Your Son, Jesus! We renounce seeking to make names for ourselves, we cast off the illusions of the world, we repent of the lusts of comfort and pleasure.

Lord, we discern and judge the spirit of Babylon. We release Your people from its drunkenness and immoralities! We line our lives up according to the standard of Your righteous judgments, that You might judge our judgment of this spirit. In Jesus' name. Amen!

CHAPTER 23

DISCERNING THE NATURE OF THE ENEMY

The Lord is uniting His people, raising up an army, equipping them, and preparing them to take their cities.

HITTING THE HEART OF YOUR ADVERSARY

In the realm of the spirit the name of an entity always corresponds to its nature. You will notice that there are many names given to the Lord in Scripture. Yet, each revealed name was actually a deeper revelation of His nature (see Genesis 22:14; Exodus 3:14). Similarly, the names of the Lord's angels are also self-descriptive.

This principle of consistency between the name and nature of spiritual beings holds true in discerning the activity and purpose of evil spirits. To defeat the rulers of darkness we must know their nature—what to expect, what their tactics are, and how they apply those tactics against our weaknesses.

In the Bible, the term *unclean spirit* is a generic term used simply to draw a distinction between angelic spirits and evil spirits. But if you want to bring deliverance, you need to know the nature of a specific unclean spirit; that is, whether the unclean spirit is a spirit of fear or sexual lust, etc. You do not need to ask it any more questions once you know its nature.

Consider that the name of the unclean spirit inhabiting the Gerasene demoniac was "Legion . . ." Why? "For we are many" (Mark 5:6–9). Knowing the name helped Jesus discern its nature, thus facilitating the actual deliverance. When John describes the fallen angel in Revelation 9:11 as the "king" over the demons in the bottomless pit, he reveals this ruler's name in Hebrew as "Abaddon, and in the Greek he has the name Apollyon." In English, these names mean "destruction" and "destroyer" respectively. Again, the name and nature match.

Once you know its nature, however, you do not need to know its name. If you were in warfare against Abaddon, you could identify the demon as the spirit of destruction (or destroyer) as readily as using the Hebrew name Abaddon. Or, you could war against it, if God so led you, by simply calling it the spirit of destruction. How do we defeat the enemy? Victory begins with the name of Jesus on our lips; it is consummated by the nature of Jesus in our hearts.

FOLLOW THE LAMB!

We have touched on a few of the enemies of God in this book. It is very important to not charge ahead, attacking principalities and powers in spiritual warfare. The first place you need to secure is your own soul. Then, as God leads, He will give strategies that are unique to your community. He will involve a number of churches and He will not send you out alone. Indeed, since Jesus warned that "any city or house divided against itself will not stand" (Matthew 12:25), the reader will do well to read our follow-up book, *The House of the Lord*, to understand the necessity of citywide unity in our war against evil.

In Scripture, we have a picture of the proper balance in all warfare: "The armies which are in heaven . . . were following Him" (see Revelation 19:11–16). In no other dimension of life will we find the phrase, "a little knowledge is a dangerous thing," more true than in spiritual warfare. If we will be victorious, we must follow Jesus as our Lord and King.

Therefore, let us be very conscious and very careful to be followers of the Lord. From our experiences, it is vital that the people in your church be trained in warfare before laying a large-scale siege against the enemy. Your attack against the strongholds of hell will be in the areas of your knowledge. Satan, on the other hand, will counterattack in the areas of your ignorance.

It is essential we understand the difference between being taught and being trained. Reading this book is being taught; being personally led by the Lord Jesus is being trained. David wrote, "He trains my hands for battle, so that my arms can bend a bow of bronze" (Psalm 18:34). This book is meant to inform you of your need for training and to provide certain insights and guidelines. What you will learn in confrontational warfare and obeying the Lord on the actual battleground will far exceed that which any book will provide. Your confidence must be securely in the Lord, not in this book.

A LAST WORD . . .

As we embrace God's eternal plan, which is to make us in the image of Christ, let us remember that no weapon formed against us shall prosper, and every tongue that accuses us in judgment we will condemn (see Isaiah 54:17). As we capture every thought unto the obedience of Christ, know with certainty, God is ready to punish all disobedience when our obedience is made complete (see 2 Corinthians 10:1–6).

Be assured, our weapons are mighty as we pray in the power of Christ's might (see Ephesians 6:10). Be confident and bold—for our prayers, like arrows, are in the heart of the King's enemies (see Psalm 45:5). Jesus Himself has gone before us; the fear of Him has the enemy's camp in disarray.

To those of you who are of the nature of Gideon, the Lord says, *Shrink not from your call, though you consider yourself but a weak, foolish or base thing, for I have chosen to use you to nullify the things that are* (see 1 Corinthians 1:28). *Rejoice and be exceedingly glad, for I Myself have purposed to consummate the battle by revelation of My fullness in your life.*

I was watching Satan fall from heaven like lightning. Behold, I have given you authority to tread upon serpents and scorpions, and over all the power of the enemy, and nothing will injure you!   —Luke 10:18–19

A SHORT GLOSSARY

"For we wrestle not against flesh and blood, but against principalities, against powers, against the rulers of the darkness of this world, against spiritual wickedness in high places" (Ephesians 6:12 KJV). The Bible mentions an order in hell, yet it is not especially clear concerning the details in its governmental system. Thus, our understanding concerning the spiritual realm comes from glimpses, not exhaustive descriptions from the Holy Writ. The following glossary represents the study and compilations made by this author. Our hope is that the definitions stated here will be found to be consistent with both the Bible and the views of our most insightful readers.

HEAVENLY PLACES

See Ephesians 3:10; 6:12.

When the Scriptures refer to heaven, they may be speaking of any of three realms which the context of the reference interprets. The first heaven is the atmospheric heaven, the sky (see Psalm 19:1). The third heaven is the most familiar definition of heaven: the realms of glory which are crowned by the highest of heavens, the dwelling place of God (see Matthew 6:9).

The heaven which is the unique object of this study is the spiritual realm which immediately surrounds planet earth and uniquely influences both the consciousness and the subconsciousness of man. It is this realm, known frequently in the Scriptures as the "heavenly places," which is the battleground of our spiritual warfare. Within this realm, good and evil spirits clash in the battle for men's souls. Ultimately, when the Lord Jesus returns and all evil is banished, this heaven will be filled with the glory of God.

DEMONS

Greek: *Daimon*.

King James wrongly translates *demons* as "devils." There is only one devil, Satan, but there are many demons. Demons were once angels "which kept not their first estate" (Jude 1:6 KJV). Demons are fallen angels (see Revelation 12:9; Matthew 25:41).

Demons differ in degrees of wickedness (see Matthew 12:45). Everything from fairies and imps to principalities and powers can be categorized as demons when the term is used generically. However, when *demon* is used as a specific term, it usually is a reference to any variety of unclean, evil spirits which not only infest mankind but also masquerade as human thoughts.

Demons are the ground troops of hell. They are the most abundant of evil spirits and, evidently, God has given them a legal right to occupy any territory that exists in defiant rebellion to God's will, including mankind. Jude 1:6 tells us that these fallen angels are kept in eternal bonds of darkness. Darkness is not merely a lightless region but a spiritual place of moral depravity.

The responsibility to "cast out demons" belongs to all believers (Mark 16:17).

DEVIL

Greek: *Diabolos*: an accuser, a slanderer. One of the names of Satan.

From this word the English word *devil* is derived, and should be applied only to Satan (Vines Expository Dictionary). (see *Satan* below)

SATAN

Greek: *Satanas,* adversary, one who resists.

The principle name of the devil, although he was first named "Lucifer" before he rebelled against God in the pre-creation universe. Satan is the slanderer of men to God and of God to men. His assault against humanity is to cause men to sin, thereby invoking the judgment of God against mankind. Our warfare against Satan is successful when we remain pure and invoke the judgment of God against the devil. One of the ministries of the Holy Spirit is to bring God's judgment against the devil (see John 16:7–11).

Satan is the ultimate source of deception and lies as well as acts of violence. Jesus said of Satan that he was a thief who came to "steal, kill and destroy" (John 10:10). Satan is the tempter. He is also the accuser of the brethren. Scripture also calls him the prince of this world and the god of this age.

This author believes that Satan himself does not appear and directly attack people in general, but the devil reserves his assault for the Lord's anointed (Job, Christ, Peter). Scripturally speaking, Satan was rebuked but not "cast out" in the manner of dealing with demons. The church successfully wars against Satan by submitting to God, living, speaking, and holding fast to the Word of God, knowing the power of Christ's sacrificial blood, and living the crucified life (see Revelation 12:10–12).

PRINCIPALITIES

See Ephesians 3:10; 6:12 KJV. Greek: *Arche.*

This word means "beginning, government, rule" and is used to describe a class of spirit-beings in the satanic hierarchy. It is likely that principalities are governmental spirits in the system of hell and that they represent the spiritual counterpart of archangels in heaven. Thus, we would assume that principalities rule over powers as well as the more numerous subcategories of demons. Principalities influence continents, countries, regions within countries, even states and major cities. It can be safely assumed that one would find these spirits presiding over places of great influence such as Hollywood, New York, Washington DC or other national capitals.

The means through which the church successfully wars against principalities is through Christ's spiritual authority and the principle of displacement. Principalities are not "cast out." Though they may exert strong influence upon individuals, they do not dwell in people; they dwell in "heavenly places." They are displaced in the spirit-realm by the ascendancy of Christ in the church and, through the church, into the community.

POWERS

See Matthew 24:29; Ephesians 6:12; 3:10 KJV.

Working with principalities, but apparently in subjection to them, are what the Bible calls "powers." The term *powers* represents both a specific class of ruling spirits and it is also a general term used to describe the entire range of ruling demonic powers, as in Matthew 24:29: "The powers of the heavens will be shaken."

It is my opinion that the energy of a power is broadcast, like radio waves over a specific territory. Thus, a power is a major demonic spirit whose primary activity is to *blanket* a given area with a particular brand of evil. They are called *powers* because that is what they are: powers of darkness. They are most likely the dark counterparts of the angelic class, virtues.

My experience has been that, during any particular week, a certain number of people would struggle with the same problems, perhaps of fear, depression or other human weakness. Once I recognized a number of similar complaints, I would pray against the specific spiritual power that characterized the common battle. It would not be long until the intensity of battle would decrease and people would, on their own, be released. The source of their battle was their individual weakness in a particular area exploited by a corresponding spiritual power. Binding that power over our geographic area, and then covering people spiritually with the blood of Jesus, caused victory to come for many of the people.

Like principalities, major powers influence the spirit realm over entire regions of countries. Different powers will work together under the control of a principality, but usually one or two will be the most influential, eventually affecting even the mannerisms of speech and general attitudes of the people in an area.

The means through which the church successfully wars against powers is through the administration of Christ's spiritual authority and the principle of displacement. Powers are not "cast out." They are displaced in the spirit-realm by the fullness of the reign of Christ in the church and through the intercessory warfare of the saints in the region.

WORLD RULERS OF DARKNESS

See Ephesians 6:12.

When the Bible speaks of the "rulers . . . of this darkness," it is speaking with reference to the highest class of principalities that, on a national and international scale, govern other principalities, as well as the powers under them.

In the book of Daniel, one such principality was known as the "prince of Persia" (see Daniel 10). Persia, at the time of Daniel's writing, was an empire that extended from eastern Europe to western India. This particular world ruler fought with the angel that was first sent in answer to Daniel's prayer. Finally, Michael, who was an archangel over Israel (equivalent to the class, *world ruler),* joined the original angel sent to Daniel and defeated the enemy.

KINGDOM OF GOD

See Mark 1:14–15; Matthew 5:3,10; 6:33.

Scripturally speaking, this phrase always refers to the eternal spiritual reality where the rule of God through Christ originates and presides. The expanse of this heavenly kingdom has two primary manifestations: heaven in eternity, and the fragrance of heaven in the realm of time, which is revealed and entered through Christ. When this author speaks of "establishing the kingdom," it is in context with the latter definition. It is not our view that the whole earth must be subdued and made subject to Christ before He returns. Rather, we speak of the kingdom of God as that dimension of eternal life which the redeemed inherit through spiritual rebirth and which the obedient discover in the meaning of Christ's words.

OTHER BOOKS
BY FRANCIS FRANGIPANE

THE POWER OF ONE CHRISTLIKE LIFE. The prayer of a Christlike intercessor is the most powerful force in the universe, delaying God's wrath until He pours out His mercy.

THE POWER OF COVENANT PRAYER. Gain the victory over the effect of curses. The section on persevering prayer is a must for anyone serious about attaining Christlikeness. The second part is the conclusion of a teaching on spiritual protection. Powerful insights on the nature of curses and how to walk in spiritual victory and freedom. (Formerly titled *The Divine Antidote*). *Published by Charisma House.*

AND I WILL BE FOUND BY YOU. The essence of *And I Will Be Found By You* is a living promise from God. If we genuinely, from our heart, pursue the Lord, He promises He will meet us. Francis calls the church to a focused season of seeking God. We must have more of God, and if it is God we desire, it is God we shall find!

THIS DAY WE FIGHT. We cannot be passive and also win the war for our souls. Pastor Frangipane exposes the disarming that occurs when we accept a passive spirit into our thoughts. The passive spirit seems innocent, yet it causes us to stop seeking God, ultimately rendering us defenseless against spiritual attack and the weaknesses of our flesh. This is essential reading for the overcoming church. *Published by Chosen Books.*

THE SHELTER OF THE MOST HIGH. Francis gives trustworthy, biblical evidence that in the midst of all our uncertainties and fears there is an available shelter from God to shield us. Once you have found this place, nothing you encounter can defeat you. This is a revised and expanded version of *The Stronghold of God*. *Published by Charisma House.*